AF729944

a country style

Some lines a day

a country style

living and creating with nature through the seasons

Harriet Thistlethwayte

MITCHELL BEAZLEY

contents

introduction

Hello, I'm Harriet and I live in rural Herefordshire with my husband Thomas, Sybil the Labrador and two recalcitrant cats. We have four children, who come and go from the house, two grandchildren and an engineering business. Who I am depends on what day of the week it is.

Some days I'm a housekeeper playing catch-up, trying to get the house ready for the next guests, who often tend to be family. Some days I'm a gardener, sowing seeds and growing flowers for the house and vegetables to eat. Some days I'm Granny, in charge of two munchkins. Other days I'm on admin duty, helping our small company run smoothly. However, perhaps my favourite days of all are the ones when I am creative: cutting fresh flowers from the garden and arranging them for the house, photographing my garden as a form of journalling, rearranging rooms and sourcing vintage pieces, or just pottering in my studio shed.

My creativity is firmly rooted in nostalgia and the romance of vintage. I haven't bought a new piece of furniture for many years – not counting kitchen units, but even those were adapted and repainted later on. I'm always searching for pieces with character and a patina that suggests a previous life. This is partly the nature of my own personal aesthetic but also for reasons of budget, and sourcing these items has always been one of my favourite pastimes.

Seasonality is hugely important to me. Growing up we only ate what was in season, and most of that came from the garden. My mother would decide what vegetable we would be eating according to what was looking good that day. Everything was home-made, from marmalade for our morning toast to a cake at teatime and pudding after our evening meal – always a pudding. Of course, I longed for white sliced bread and a packet of biscuits, but they were considered a frivolous waste of money and also not really *proper* food. How ahead of her time my mother was. I've only recently realized this, but to her it was simply the way you lived in the country.

Some of her philosophy became ingrained in me. I have always made bread, even though, once we had children, the odd sliced loaf did slip in. I grew vegetables, too. But Mum's monthly visit to the supermarket became weekly for me and then gradually even more frequent – it was all so convenient, so why not eat food in which some or all of the work had been done for you? Then, about 20 years ago, I came home

Right: Standing in the doorway of the greenhouse, which we renovated in 2019. I have vivid childhood memories of watching and helping as my mother sowed seeds and grew plants for the vegetable patch and garden in here.

from Nottinghamshire, to look after Mum when she was recovering from an operation for a replacement ankle, which had completely incapacitated her. I was glad to repay some of the kindness she had shown me when the children were little and she endlessly had them to stay in the holidays. Completely in charge of running the house, I experienced for the first time what it was like to live like her, and it changed everything for me. I had to cook with what was available in the garden; instead of starting with a recipe, I started with the produce and then decided what to cook with it. Contrary to what I was expecting, it wasn't limiting, it was freeing, and I wasn't wasting precious time trudging round the supermarket. Pudding meant wandering up to the orchard in the soft, late-afternoon light to pick some apples. There are so many ways to cook apples.

I became mindful of the minute changes in the garden and fields. Instead of watching TV, I watched nature, read books and pottered. I looked outwards instead of inwards. Without the stresses and trials of my everyday life I had time to think – time to experience the shift in the light, the burnishing of the leaves as they prepared for autumn. I suppose I was experiencing what they call 'slow living'. I knew that I wanted the rest of my life to be more like that, and not just when I was with my parents.

In 2011, by pure happenstance, my mother and father were looking to downsize at the same time that we wanted to relocate from the north of England to be within easy travelling distance of both sets of parents. When my husband suggested moving to the house I grew up in, I was very unsure about it. Would it somehow be a step back in my life? Would I be expected to step into my mother's shoes and be as big a part of the community as she had been, with all the committee meetings and commitments that entailed?

Left: The intentional blurring between the edges of the garden and the fields around it is never more obvious than in May, when cow parsley is encouraged to grow where it wants.

And then there was the garden – an immaculate 3.2 hectares (8 acres) that she had spent the previous 45 years filling with rare plants, which she tended to on a daily basis. I had always grown vegetables and loved working in the small borders of whatever house we were living in at the time, but running a household with four children and a regularly absent husband meant that the garden came fairly far down on my must-do list.

However, the house itself was a lovely Georgian farmhouse with beautiful proportions, which I already knew I loved. It had the bonus of being completely unspoiled in that it had hardly changed at all since my parents had moved in. With its rudimentary central heating and ancient electrics, it was known as a house where you always had to add an extra layer – or two – of clothing when you visited. So we knew that whatever happened in the garden, first we had a sizable updating job on our hands. Despite the nightmares that we'd be taking on far too much at the time in our lives when most people want to start doing a little less, we took the decision to move into my childhood home.

About a week after we had moved in, on a hot July day, I took some time out from unpacking to wander alone around the garden. The air was warm and I walked quietly, absorbing sounds and smells, and I was struck by how contented I felt despite the upheaval of the move. The word 'home' came to me, and I realized that was it: I was home, not just physically but mentally, too. In all the other houses we'd lived in during 28 years of marriage, when we were always searching for something I couldn't even articulate, I had never felt like this – I knew that at last I was where I could be truly content.

This is the story of how I live now that I'm home.

Right: The place I call home, and the flowers I grow here. In contrast to when my parents gardened the plot, there is now a wild-flower meadow, replete with wild carrot in midsummer. Daisies grow abundantly and nasturtiums are encouraged to sprawl.

KDW 44F
GB

about @yomargey

About ten years ago, a friend of mine told me I should be posting my photographs on a platform called Instagram. I had always loved using a camera and, when the children were small, I had studied photography – including developing and printing film – in evening classes.

I was sceptical about social media to begin with, as I was not sure that I wanted to be part of that world. When I finally did begin to post my pictures, however, I realized that it was the perfect outlet for creativity. Whereas I had seemed to spend most of my time doing things for other people, this was something that I could do just for me. What's more, I didn't even need to leave home and it didn't cost a penny.

To my surprise, people seemed to like my pictures, and I enjoyed interacting with them. Making friendships, both virtual and real, has been a wonderful bonus. Once you've found your tribe on Instagram, you are provided with ready-made friends who have similar passions – people who enjoy looking around gardens and growing and arranging flowers, then photographing them and chatting about it.

People say they come to my account for the sense of calm it gives them. The restricted colour palette that I use might be part of the reason for this, I think, and the sense of nostalgic simplicity that these snippets of my life provide. I don't do this simply as my online aesthetic, it is part of how I live and reflects a battle against overwhelm that I work on constantly – not always the easiest thing to achieve with social media.

On the positive side, Instagram has reawakened my love of photography. They say contentment is about finding joy in little things, and photography teaches you to notice small changes and subtle shifts. Being outside with my camera has helped to ground me and bring me closer to the natural world. So, despite its challenges, I will always be grateful for my Instagram family, with whom I can interact from the comfort of my kitchen.

Left: A selection of posts from @yomargey, showing snippets of my life I lead, aided by two cats, a dog and a greenhouse.

the greenhouse

If you follow me on Instagram it's possibly because of the greenhouse, which has always garnered a lot of attention. It is at the back of the house, just outside the kitchen. It still has two dessert vines, one white and one black, which we believe are the original ones, planted when it was first built in 1900.

The greenhouse probably also had peaches and other hothouse fruit trees in there, because of the huge heating pipes that still remain, sadly redundant now. When my parents moved here, there was a small boiler-house underneath the vinery, reached by steps that descended behind it. A boiler, no doubt kept fired up all winter, was manned by a lad, part of a gardening team that at one time, we were told, consisted of nine full-time gardeners. The boiler was beyond repair when my parents moved in and, slightly wistfully, they filled in the little room and took away the steps.

Over the years, my father made several repairs to the greenhouse, some more successful than others, and it often leaked. I have happy memories of spring lunches in there when I visited with my children in the holidays. By June it would be too hot at midday to spend time in. As the years went by, it became increasingly decrepit and, shortly after we moved here, my husband propped up the frame inside with a single large post. We carried on for a bit, with slight trepidation every time we stepped inside.

By 2018, we had decided something had to be done. Every time there was a gale in the forecast we crossed our fingers, knowing we would probably lose a few more panes. Having finally finished most of the house renovations, the pot for building work was a little light, to say the least, and anyway, how would we go about it? We knew we didn't want a modern greenhouse in its place, and how could we afford to build a copy of what was there? We sadly agreed that we might just have to knock it down. Luckily, Bernie came to the rescue – the man who has been such a godsend to us, helping us repair the sash windows in the house – always treading lightly, whatever he worked on, keen to disturb the house as little as possible. He had worked for Mum and Dad when they lived here, replacing the rotten parts of doors and windows – a truly skilled carpenter.

Bernie agreed, with Thomas's help, to reconstruct the vinery from the brick level upwards exactly as it had been originally, in cedar. They worked together slowly and methodically for most of the summer of 2019, and by early autumn it was finished. I managed to find some Victorian legs for staging to go down one side of the interior. The fig growing along the back wall didn't seem much the worse for wear after being covered in limewash, and the vines miraculously survived intact, too. I bought a large second-hand teak table on eBay and it was ready to be a usable space again. Little did we know that the following March the country would go into lockdown and two of our four children, plus two grandchildren, would come and live with us. That spring the vinery came into its own as the place where we ate every evening, candles lit and fairy lights glowing.

Left: The greenhouse, surrounded by the abundance of June, with white pelargoniums filling the staging. It is a favourite setting for a summer evening meal.

Top left: The original greenhouse, although romantic, had become unstable.
Below left: During the renovation, my husband spent much time, some of it precariously perched, thinking about the best way to proceed.
This page: The glory of July, when we enjoy outdoor living as much as possible.

spring

The garden is never really asleep. Even in the coldest months there is activity – hidden from view but happening all the same. Dark grey days can discourage us from spending time outside, with fingers becoming numb all too quickly when doing anything that doesn't involve brisk activity.

Then one day, usually at the beginning of March, there is an almost indefinable difference in the air as you step out of the house. There is an embracing warmth, but also the scent of fresh growth, of winter blossom warmed by the sun. Spring is heralded by a hundred small changes and here, in my favourite season, we begin the gardening year.

All of the plans and dreams set down in winter can now be put into practice. The mood is exuberant; there is new growth every day as the borders begin to flourish. The season also brings a sudden surge of gardening jobs. Work done now in keeping weeds at bay will pay dividends for your young plants. Paths are pleasingly clear, for a short while at least, and it can be satisfying to take a walk at the end of the lengthening days to admire what you have achieved.

Right: Some of the earliest spring blooms to enjoy – hellebores and primroses, one sculptural and impressive and the other small and simple. Hellebores are among the first pickings for vases; their long growing season means they can accompany spring bulbs out of the greenhouse.

grow your own

There is never a bad time to become more self-sufficient, but perhaps right now there is a particular need for it. With threats of food shortages, as well as the vagaries of climate change affecting harvests and supply chains, being able to grow at least some of your food can provide the sort of security that hasn't seemed necessary for many decades.

Being able to cook yourself a meal with ingredients from your garden is not only very satisfying, it's also good for the planet. Your home-grown food will be pesticide-free. What is more, it will taste so much better than anything that has been sitting in a chilled warehouse. Gardening's benefits to mental health have been well documented; just 15 minutes pottering outside, nurturing plants, will lift the spirits immeasurably. Could growing vegetables be the epitome of self-care? Growing plants can feed the mind, body and soul, while helping the planet at the same time.

As with all gardening, however, it isn't always plain sailing. In recent years, at least in some areas of the British countryside, the large population of deer has become something of an issue for gardeners. Fresh green shoots being irresistible to them, they can strip a garden of new growth overnight – a very distressing sight to wake up to. For us, living in the lee of woodland, their natural habitat, this problem is greatly increased. To counter this we built an 8-foot-high (2.4-metre) fence with 4-inch treated posts and black half-inch netting stapled to the posts. A simple netting-covered gate at one end opens to allow me and my wheelbarrow through. The fence has the added bonus of keeping out rabbits. Knowing that my vegetables are safe from marauders has encouraged me to grow so many different types. Celery was a revelation to me – so superior in taste to what is available in shops. Indeed if you grow vegetables for one reason only, do it for the flavour.

Above: The secure compound known as the vegetable patch. **Right:** Summer produce from the garden and greenhouse supply our every meal. Kale is probably my most used vegetable; we eat it raw in salads, chopped finely and tossed through pasta, or as part of a winter stew. In fact, it is the stalwart of the winter garden.

sowing vegetable seeds

Now is the time for sowing seeds in earnest. Although it is possible to start seeds in February with the help of a propagator, they are fragile and can get leggy, only to be wiped out by a heavy March frost. It is better to begin a little later, because the plants will grow more quickly; as they aren't continually searching for light, they will also be sturdier.

The first vegetables to sow now, either in a greenhouse or a windowsill, are salad vegetables. A seed mix of cut-and-come-again vegetables is a useful starting point. There is such an array of seeds available online and in garden centres that choosing can be a bit of a minefield. I go for a selection that includes milder leaves and a spicy mix, as well as rocket.

It is important to sow little and often, to avoid the hunger gap when suddenly your first crop has gone to seed but the next lot are only a few millimetres (an eighth of an inch) high. Sowing every three weeks or so should prevent this, but it is surprisingly hard to achieve as the weeks speed up and the demands on us from the garden increase. Luckily, as there is more light in the day, seeds germinate and grow more rapidly, and it isn't long before a new crop is ready to be picked.

Also ready to sow are tomatoes, cucumbers and chillies. If there isn't room to grow all of these, I recommend growing a chilli plant on a windowsill. These are easy to nurture and very productive, and will be on hand when you need to add a little spice to your cooking. Generally speaking, the larger the chilli, the milder the flavour. I like to grow several different varieties and so I usually sow one or two packets of seed and then buy a few small plants of different varieties. You don't really want 15 identical plants, and those tiny seeds soon grow, taking up a lot of valuable space.

Above: The thrill of the tiny seed that arrives in February and becomes something you can eat by summer never gets old.
Left: Winter greens on their journey to providing nourishment and flavour on a cold January day.

plant swap

It is worth finding out about local plant swaps, held in village or town halls, where gardeners can bring their surplus seeds and young plants and take away something new to grow that has been donated by a fellow gardener. Excess plants also make great gifts for friends – they could be my favourite sort of present to receive!

It's better to sow only a few seeds and then either swap plants with friends who are growing different varieties or take them to one of the swap fairs that pop up in village halls everywhere in spring. Not only are these great places to meet new friends and gardeners, but they are also good opportunities to learn from seasoned growers, who are nearly always more than happy to share their long-garnered knowledge and give advice. Added to this, you can come away with a few plants and packets of seeds, all for free. Gardening is a community pastime – you may be toiling away on your own but there will nearly always be someone else close by doing the same who is happy to give advice and chat about things you are both interested in. A local gardening club is also a great way of meeting like-minded folk, and going on adventures to other gardens in a group can be fun. In fact, an advantage of this is that you get to see private gardens that are not normally open to the public but that welcome small groups. Facebook is a good source for finding out about gardening clubs and plant swaps.

Above: A tray of lettuce seedlings, ready to be pricked out into individual plugs on their journey to the outside garden. **Right:** I divided a nepeta in early spring to create extra plants, now ready to be taken as a gift to a friend.

NEPETA

creating a small cut-flower patch

To have a flow of fresh flowers for the house, it's a good idea to create a dedicated area for growing flowers specifically for cutting. This way you don't have to denude your borders all the time. Some annuals, such as cosmos and sweet peas, positively benefit from being picked regularly, but it can feel a little brutal picking from a border when there are only a few blooms.

Flowers in the house are such a mood lifter – they really bring a room alive. Punctuating the year with what is blooming at a particular time, they help to root us in the season. There are tulips in spring (not January, as the supermarkets would have us believe), dahlias in late summer and autumn, roses in June. By using flowers truly seasonally, and not according to some weird manufactured seasons that have more to do with profit than nature, we connect ourselves to the natural world, becoming more aware of its rhythms. By leaning into the ebb and flow of the months, we tether ourselves to a healthier life, which can benefit us in so many ways. You don't need a huge amount of space for a cut-flower patch – in fact, I have grown enough cosmos to pick all summer in two large pots. However, pots do require frequent watering. If you have room, a patch of ground measuring roughly 3 x 2 metres (10 x 6 feet 6 inches) will enable you to grow a rotation of blooms for picking. Another option is a raised bed, which is easier on your back. The optimum size is 3 x 1.2 metres (10 x 4 feet) – any wider and it becomes difficult to reach the centre. One raised bed with succession planting would be enough for a weekly vase of flowers, or several vases in the summer months. A bunch of blooms also makes a wonderful gift.

Left: The cutting patch in midsummer.
Above: Tulips are succeeded by dahlias in this bed; the wooden frame constructed out of hazel sticks is needed to support them as they grow. This will last for about five years before needing to be replaced, with little-to-no maintenance needed in the meantime.

annuals to grow

A cold winter's evening is the perfect time to browse seed catalogues, dream of spring and decide what to grow next season. You might be attracted to certain colours and make your selections on that basis, or be drawn to old-fashioned cottage-garden varieties. There are a wide range of annuals to choose from, but the following are some of my favourites.

Bishop's flower (*Ammi majus*): Similar to cow parsley but more refined, *Ammi majus* is such a useful flower. With its clouds of delicate umbels (above, with the butterfly), it looks good on its own but also adds a cohesion to a group of other blooms, owing to its feathery foliage and small clusters of tiny blooms. Each flower-head is a mini work of art, such is its beauty. The seeds are quick to germinate in spring under cover but can also be sown in autumn without heat to create well-established plants by the following spring. A benefit of this flower is that it self-seeds, so it is a good border plant, returning every year.

Corncockle (*Agrostemma*): Another magnet for bees and butterflies, this is one of my favourite flowers to grow every year. I find the blooms (the larger white flowers shown above) astonishingly beautiful, as if an artist had used a fine liner to draw the perfectly radiating dotted lines that emerge from the centre. Once picked, they lend a delicate, airy look to a bouquet. They can be sown direct in a border in late summer or early spring, but also under glass if preferred.

Honeywort (*Cerinthe major*): A bee-friendly flower, with deep purple blooms and grey-green foliage, Cerinthe adds drama and a sculptural quality to a vase. Easy to grow, it can be sown indoors throughout spring and summer. The seeds are large and so handy to harvest. Yet they also self-seed freely and are relatively hardy. I only need to sow a few of these every year to maintain a constant supply of flowers.

Cosmos (*Cosmos Bipannatus*): This is always a favourite. If I could grow only one annual, it would be this. Some years I dally with yellow or pink, but always go back to white, of which 'Purity' is the best variety in my opinion. It can be sown under cover in late March, or earlier with heat. I sow into a small seed tray and then pot on a few weeks later. This is followed by pinching out the tips to stop them becoming leggy and make them bushy instead. It helps to keep the young plants in a cold frame to acclimatize them slowly. After being left outside in their pots for a week to be hardened off, they can be planted out in mid-May.

Pot marigold (*Calendula officinalis*): Such an easy flower to grow for fairly instant satisfaction, calendula comes in shades from bright orange and yellow to more subtle pale yellows. The flowers have the bonus of being edible, and the petals look so pretty when scattered over a summer salad. Sow indoors in trays – the seeds germinate at 18–20°C (64–68°F). They can also be sown outdoors in mid-spring once the soil has warmed up. They benefit from deadheading to encourage more flowers and will continue to bloom until the first frost.

Nasturtium (*Tropaeolum Majus*): These pretty flowers are perhaps the easiest of all to grow, which may be the reason so many of us grew them as children. They are now definitely back in fashion, and new colours are constantly being introduced. From the palest yellow 'Milkmaid' to deep-red 'Black Velvet', there is a huge range to choose from. I love varieties with variegated leaves, which, being edible, look pretty in salads, while their flavour adds a mustardy zing. They self-seed freely and might need editing the following year, but I mostly allow them to roam where they want.

displaying spring bulbs

Early spring can still be a quiet time for flowers in the garden, so the pots of bulbs that were planted in autumn are a good way of bringing early colour. I have pots in the greenhouse and on my outdoor table. This means I have a long flowering season, as everything blooms about three weeks earlier in the greenhouse. A sunny windowsill would also produce early blooms.

From narcissi and muscari to hyacinths and snakeshead fritillaries, there are so many spring bulbs to choose from. I can tend towards overexcitement at ordering time, but I never seem to have too many. At a time when the garden is only just waking up, these early spring bulbs bring a treasured joy.

After blooming, when they have died back a little, I snip off the flower head but not the leaves, and then I plant them out into the garden to continue their life there. A grassy area is best for daffodils and narcissi, where they can fade happily without spoiling the look of a border. Hyacinths get put in the hellebore border, where they bloom a little later in the year and end up looking a bit less extravagant and more in keeping with their positioning out in the garden.

Snakeshead fritillaries thrive in much damper soil than other bulbs, their natural habitat being water meadows, where they can look quite magical en masse. If you can find a slightly soggy area in the garden, they multiply generously once established.

Left: Grouping narcissi of similar colour together gives a cohesive look. 'Tête-à-tête' are one of the first to flower.
Above: A queen bumblebee has flown sleepily into the greenhouse for a much-needed meal.

This page: The plant table near the kitchen door, covered in spring bulbs including muscari, hellebores, hyacinths and various narcissi.
Right: The display in the greenhouse includes *N.* 'Tête-à-tête' and *N. bulbocodium*, the enchanting 'petticoat daffodil'.

tulip time

With each passing week, growth becomes more noticeable, as greenery flourishes. Before we know it, flower picking can begin in earnest. There are now enough blooms to be more generous in arrangements. Tulip time brings drama and glamour to every vase. On the terrace outside the kitchen I grow mostly white tulips, but in the cutting garden I like a variety of peachy tones with some very dark colours.

A favourite tulip is 'La Belle Epoque' – with its muted tones, it mixes well with other flowers and has an appealing antique quality, which matches vintage furniture and fabric perfectly. Tulips have suffered a little in recent years with tulip fire, a fungal disease that distorts the leaves and stunts growth. I grow far fewer than I used to, but that is also because they are loved by deer. I would suggest not cramming bulbs into pots in the way known as 'bulb lasagne', which has been so fashionable. With a little more space between bulbs there is less opportunity for disease to develop.

It's hard to imagine a spring without any tulips at all, but a few pots are enough to keep me happy.

If deer are a problem, place pots close to the house and in particular close to a doorway where there is a lot of footfall; this has the added benefit of being there for you to enjoy as soon as you open the door. Bulbs can be bought anytime from September but planting them should be delayed until November or December to give them the best chance of escaping disease (and also of being dug up by a mischievous squirrel).

Above: White tulips in pots outside the kitchen door, where I can enjoy them every day. I like a restricted colour palette, providing a calm outlook for the sometimes harassed cook.

Right: All other tulips are grown in the safety of the fenced-in cutting patch, which is where these *T.* 'Belle Epoque' started life.

Blossom can be one of the easiest ways to transform a room. You don't even need to arrange it – a single stem in a tall vase can bring life to a space. In fact, less is more with blossom, as each stem has an abundance of blooms, so it's easy to make a statement with very little work. It won't last for a particularly long time once cut, but I find the falling petals only add to the charm. It also looks lovely mixed with tulips in a vase, bringing a delicate contrast to their flamboyance.

a spring wreath

By the middle of March there is real evidence of growth, particularly in the hedgerow, and this can be a great place to begin foraging for pieces to make a spring wreath. This isn't on the grand scale of an autumn wreath or with the flamboyance of a summer one. A spring wreath is more compact, as befitting the sparseness of available material, but has a delightful simplicity.

1 Start out with a basic wreath ring (see An Autumn Wreath, page 130), then assemble your flowers. Blackthorn blossom, with its small, perfectly shaped white flowers, is a good starting point. To create balance, match its delicate blooms with small-leafed plants. Evergreen euonymus is such a useful shrub to grow for winter/spring foliage, as is cotoneaster. I have also used *Cornus mas* blossom, but yellow hamamelis would be a good substitute. Finally, some willow, which is just coming into leaf, provides the zingiest green, and some beech, which is not yet in leaf, provides a structural element.

2 Cut your chosen stems to varying lengths and start winding them in bunches of three around your wreath ring. Starting at the top and working in an anticlockwise direction, place them diagonally on the ring and bind them to it with florist's wire or simple twine. Pull the wire tightly to ensure that your bunches will not come loose.

3 Continue in this way around the wreath ring, checking for visual balance as you do.

4 When you are happy with the arrangement of the foliage, hang up the wreath with either a ribbon or, as I prefer, a piece of twine. Spray the wreath regularly with water to keep it fresh for as long as possible.

a spring table

Easter is often the first moment since Christmas when friends gather to celebrate and eat a special meal. The 'hunker down' mentality of winter, when I want only a small group to eat with us, is shrugged off. Suddenly I feel re-energized and expansive, and experience once again the need to share life and food with those I love.

Creating an Easter table is a joyful moment, with the knowledge that the cold of winter is behind us and the pleasures of summer ahead. I lay a cloth over the table – my favourite for this time of year is striped in green, with a ruffled edge. If I am joining two or more tables together I use a selection of old white sheets. Down the centre of the table I place as many slim glass vases and bottles as I can fit. They are all different heights and sizes – I'm not looking for a uniform look, but something more whimsical. Into each bottle go two or three stems, though some might have only one, which is okay, as the feeling of abundance is created by the amount of bottles.

Crockery and glassware can be matching or not, usually depending on how many guests will be present. There is always a theme – for Easter it is usually floral. I like to combine etched water glasses with bowls and plates of the sort my parents used when they were first married – I am so glad I kept these during the big clear-out when we moved. It is far less stuffy to have a mix of patterns that, while making a cohesive whole, appear more relaxed and inviting.

Left: I gathered these small bottles – some were sauce bottles in a former life – over time. I've been known to buy a particular condiment because of the shape of the bottle rather than its contents.

GOLDEN AGE
PRIDE AND PREJUDICE
JANE AUSTEN
FISHERMAN'S KNOTS & WRINKLES
Through the Looking-Glass

the joy of junking

Sourcing vintage items for my home and work as a photographer is one of my favourite things to do. I try to avoid buying new pieces, partly for sustainability but also because I love the charm that a preloved item can have – a history that shows itself in patina. There's a story in that worn surface, and I will add my own narrative to it while I am its custodian.

It's not all about larger pieces of furniture; smaller items, too, can become part of a treasured collection. A studio pottery bowl lovingly made by hand, or an old wooden photo frame that has seen several reincarnations, is the sort of thing I search for that gives me so much pleasure. A large part of it is about creating a look that is unique to me and the search is half of the adventure. Pieces I buy have my story attached to them already because of where I found them and who I was with at the time. A day spent 'junking', as my husband calls it, is one of my favourite days out.

Junking is best undertaken with a companion, as searching for items that one of you 'really needs' and then spotting the exact thing you are looking for, which has been overlooked by everyone else, adds a layer of pleasure and shared excitement. I'm very lucky in that my eldest daughter loves days like these, being similarly 'afflicted', as my husband likes to put it. We have shared many happy days at antique fairs and in vintage shops. I also seem to unknowingly be drawn to people with the same tendency – several of my closest friends enjoy the search, too. It is such a great way to spend an afternoon catching up on news in-between the 'oh, look at that, I can't leave that here looking so sad.' Cradling our booty, we happily make our way home.

When buying vintage, I stick primarily to natural materials, like wood, because of the texture but also the character. I also prefer items to be handmade – you can feel the love and work that have gone into something handmade. It has a personality all of its own, which can sometimes be lacking in something machine-made. However, I don't strictly adhere to this rule – if the item is factory-made and has visible signs of use, which over the years will have given it its own personality, that can also be very pleasing.

Lastly, it is important to be selective. Pieces have to resonate with me to be worth buying. I am not hoarding, which just leads to clutter – we are adding to a display that we will walk past every day. Or I might choose something seasonal, such as a vintage decoration that will be brought out every year to be enjoyed. Finally, if you do see something that lights up your imagination and sparks that feeling, you must buy it there and then. A few times I have thought that I will go back for a piece at the end of a search, only to find it has been snapped up by someone else in the meantime.

Left: There is so much to love at Wye Valley Vintage (see page 218). This sort of display makes my heart skip a beat: candle holders, enamelware and small board paintings.

Previous pages, left: A pretty display of blossom, books and collected items on a small bookcase, to celebrate the season.

Previous pages, right: A table centrepiece, simply constructed on a small wreath ring that has been covered with moss from the garden, tied on to keep it secure. After winding pieces of ivy around, I simply poked in some forget-me-nots and narcissi. Misting the moss with water will help to keep the blooms fresh.

There are several places to enjoy searching for pieces to collect. The greatest range of objects is found at an antiques and vintage fair, also known as a flea market or collectors' fair. These are usually held at large showgrounds, which always seem to be noticeably colder than the surrounding area, so a word of warning: wrap up well! I can remember going to one with my husband with one woolly hat between us – we took it in turns to wear it for ten minutes each, while the piercing wind whistled around us. There is no greater buzzkill than feeling too cold while junking in a draughty aircraft hangar, so I usually go armed with several layers of clothes to add or remove as the situation demands.

Below: An outdoor antiques fair or flea market can be a great day out, especially if it has the beautiful surroundings of the Malvern Hills, as this one does. **Right:** I can always find time to mooch around in a vintage store like this one.

You may find your greatest bargains at a collectors' fair, especially if you can dare to leave it until nearly the end of the show, when the stallholders will not want the job of lugging all their wares home with them and will be much more amenable to a reduced offer. You're treading a thin line here between success and disappointment, as there is the potential for someone else to buy that treasure that was meant to be yours, which can be very upsetting! Whatever time you go, it's always sensible to ask if there is movement on the price – the stallholder will be expecting it and has probably already included a little leeway in the asking price. It can be hard initially to have the confidence to ask for 'the best price' or 'the death', as it is somewhat alarmingly known, on a piece. It's not the end of the world if they say no, and then you just have to decide if it's worth it to you. Never forget, you can always walk away (and then return later on, after all). In fact, most vendors will offer a little discount, it being a part of the dance between buyer and seller that is as old as time, and part of the charm of junking.

My local collectors' fair is based at the Three Counties Showground in Malvern, Worcestershire, where it is held every month in the spring and summer. Similar fairs are held at Newbury, Shepton Mallet and, the original and largest of all, at Newark (see page 218).

Next there are antiques warehouses, usually in disused Victorian factories, aircraft hangars or even farm sheds. They, too, can be cold and draughty, so wrap up warm. Expect to pay more for pieces here, and with much less haggling room. If 'NT' appears on the ticket, it stands for 'no trade' and means you won't get a discount. However, it's always worth asking, especially if you are buying more than one piece from the same seller. These emporiums often have a small coffee shop, an excellent spot to refuel with coffee and cake, giving you essential thinking time to decide whether a piece is or is not for you.

A few towns have a relatively large number of antique shops and are therefore well worth a visit for a happy day out. Our nearest in North Herefordshire is Leominster, which has a wealth of purveyors of vintage items. It also has a couple of reclamation yards, which are good hunting grounds. Hungerford in Berkshire is another town filled with antique shops, as is Tetbury in Gloucestershire, although the prices here may induce a sharp intake of breath, mostly being aimed at those with deep pockets.

Some shops sell a carefully curated selection of new pieces and also have a vintage section. Our closest is Baileys Home and Garden Store, a place friends coming

Left: A vintage French schoolteacher's desk that I found on Facebook Marketplace; it now lives in my potting shed, where the patina and marks on the old wooden top complement the stone walls. I made a curtain for the base from some leftover fabric.

to stay always want to visit. It's as much about theatre as a shopping experience. Filling you with a sense of awe as soon as you step in, it is altogether a sensory experience. Another favourite is Wye Valley Vintage, a few miles from Ross-on-Wye: a beautifully curated collection of all things vintage. Domestic Science in Nailsworth is close by, too. With branches in Stow-on-the-Wold and Tetbury as well, their cleverly curated display will immediately enchant and delight.

I'm a big fan of charity shops. There can be an awful lot of tat to sift through, but they are places where you could find a real bargain if you are lucky.

Car boot sales are also famous for the odd find that ends up on the TV series *Antiques Roadshow* because it was bought for pennies but turns out to be worth thousands. The early start has always been a bit off-putting for me, but if you like being up with the lark, there's sure to be a car booty in your nearest town.

Finally, you could try junking from the comfort of your sofa. Both eBay and Facebook Marketplace can be great hunting grounds. Remember to take into account the shipping costs, which may be substantial. If you have to collect the item yourself, restrict your search area to how far you are prepared to travel, taking into account fuel money. That said, it is where I have found my greatest bargains. This isn't usually the place for haggling, but people often want to get rid of pieces quickly and will therefore price them very reasonably. Oh, the thrill of a bargain – it never seems to get old.

Above: Another charming display at Wye Valley Vintage. **Right:** I was immediately attracted to the chipped and worn surface of this cupboard, which I found online. Removing it from a small cottage and onto the back of our truck entailed quite a struggle, as it was extremely heavy – happily, a mark of something well constructed.

spring recipes

A spell of warm weather can make us believe that we are nearing summer, only for frosts to return the following week. It's still early days in the produce year, but rhubarb, especially the early varieties, can be abundant and useful for so much more than crumbles. Foraging for wild garlic can be fun with little people, often to make pesto but here I use it in soup. My recipe for everyday bread is a staple in our household, not surprisingly considering how often toast is the basis for a very quick and satisfying meal.

wild garlic soup

The days can still be chilly at this time of year, and if I've spent the morning in the garden or out and about on a junking expedition, I'll need something warming when I return. That something is usually soup. Served with a hunk of crusty bread, it's both comforting and sustaining. Wild garlic grows abundantly in my area, and I do love a foraged meal, but if you can't get your hands on any, you could easily substitute it with watercress or baby spinach.

Serves 4, or 2 hungry people

- 25g (1oz) butter
- 1 onion, finely chopped
- 2 medium potatoes, peeled and cut into 1cm (½ inch) cubes
- 1 litre (1¾ pints) vegetable stock
- 200g (7oz) wild garlic leaves, roughly chopped
- salt and pepper
- double cream, to serve

Melt the butter in a large saucepan over a medium heat. Add the onion and give it a stir. Then add the potatoes, season with salt and pepper and stir well. Reduce the heat, cover the pan and leave the vegetables to cook gently for 10–15 minutes, or until soft.

Pour in the stock and bring to the boil, then stir in the wild garlic and cook for 2 minutes until wilted. Liquidize with a stick blender, then warm through over a low heat, adjusting the seasoning if necessary. Serve with a swirl of cream.

everyday bread

The problem with making bread is that once you get the hang of it, going back to buying the stuff is very hard. It is so much better than the preservative-filled pap available on the shelves that it's hard to justify not making it. My mother always made bread, and I seem to have inherited the practice. Over the years, I've dallied with sourdough and various other recipes, but this is the one I always come back to.

I should say here that it's important for the bread that you use strong white flour, to provide the gluten strength needed for the maximum rise. Using all brown flour doesn't work as well, however tempting it is to try, as the finished loaf can edge towards the dreaded 'brick' territory, which is never good! I like to use seeded brown bread flour, but it's entirely your choice.

Makes 2 loaves

- 500g (1lb 2oz) strong white bread flour, plus extra for dusting
- 500g (1lb 2oz) strong brown bread flour
- 1 tablespoon salt
- 2 tablespoons caster sugar
- 2 x 7g (¼oz) sachets fast-action dried yeast
- 550ml (19fl oz) tepid water
- vegetable oil, for greasing (I use the type that comes as a spray)

Put all the ingredients except the oil into a large mixing bowl and stir with a fork until they start to come together, at which point you can go in with your hands and mix until you have a very sticky ball of dough. Turn out on to a clean work surface and knead, stretching and rolling the dough to strengthen the gluten, until you have a smooth, soft ball. You may need to add a little more flour or a drop more water during this process to achieve the right consistency.

Place the dough in a lightly oiled bowl and cover with a large plastic bag – I keep one purely for this purpose, but I have also been known to use a shower cap. Leave in a warm spot, or at least one away from any draughts, until it has doubled in size, which could be up to 2 hours.

Grease two 450g (1lb) loaf tins.

Uncover the dough and knock it back by punching the air out of it. Divide in half and shape each half so that there is smooth dough at the top, then place in the oiled tins. Return to the warm spot, this time covered with a clean tea towel, and leave until the dough has risen above the top of each tin, which can take between 30 minutes and 1 hour depending on the warmth of the proving spot.

Meanwhile, preheat the oven to 180°C (350°F), Gas Mark 4.

Place the loaf tins carefully in the oven – any knocks at this stage can be fatal – and bake for 45 minutes. The tops should be nicely browned and the smell enticing. Remove from the oven immediately and gently turn the loaves out of their tins. Place on a wire rack to cool for as long as you can bear to wait, ideally at least 20 minutes, but 5 minutes will do.

rhubarb cake

After a long, productive day in the garden taking advantage of the warmer spring weather, it is a delight to stop for a slice of cake and a cup of tea, while resting your back and gazing with satisfaction on all your hard work. Rhubarb always signifies spring to me, as it is the first crop to be harvested and cooked, and its beautiful pink colour is such a boost after the grey of winter.

Serves 10

- 1 lemon
- 180g (6¼oz) caster sugar
- 4 or 5 rhubarb stalks, trimmed
- 2 large eggs
- 100g (3½oz) Greek yoghurt
- 90ml (6 tablespoons) mild olive oil, plus extra for greasing
- 170g (6oz) plain flour
- 120g (4¼oz) ground almonds
- 1 teaspoon baking powder
- pinch of salt
- flaked almonds, to decorate

Preheat the oven to 180°C (350°F), Gas Mark 4. Grease a 23cm (9in) round springform cake tin.

Grate the zest of the lemon into a large mixing bowl, add 100g (3½oz) of the sugar and mix together. Set aside.

Slice one of the rhubarb stalks diagonally to decorate the top of the cake and place in a small bowl with 1 tablespoon of the remaining caster sugar and a squeeze of juice from the zested lemon. Dice the rest of the rhubarb into another bowl and mix with 3 more tablespoons of the sugar and another squeeze of lemon juice.

Whisk the eggs, yoghurt and olive oil into the bowl containing the lemon-sugar mixture. Add the flour, ground almonds, baking powder and salt and mix together gently. Stir in the diced rhubarb.

Scrape the cake batter into the tin. Top with the sliced rhubarb, either haphazardly or in a pretty pattern. Sprinkle over the remaining sugar and the flaked almonds. Bake for 40–50 minutes, or until a sharp knife inserted into the cake comes out clean. Remove from the oven and allow to cool completely in the tin on a wire rack. Run a sharp knife around the edge of the tin before releasing the cake from the tin.

summer

The sharp lines in the garden have lost their definition, as foliage and flowers tumble over edges and down steps. The air has a tangible warmth even at 7am, and there is an exuberance and abundance to the garden. Suddenly there are more courgettes than you can eat. Summer has arrived.

A walk around the garden early in the morning can be the most precious part of the day. With only a cup of coffee and birdsong for company, this is a time when I look at everything and enjoy the view without thinking about the jobs ahead or the to-do list. For this moment I am a human being rather than a human doing, and it is a time to be treasured.

Right: Summer moments around the garden, as foxgloves reach their peak, the meadow garden is full of daisies and cow parsley grows abundantly at the field edges. With open windows all round, we relish summer.

the summer vegetable patch

As the weather warms up, there comes a time when the risk of frost is behind us and tender vegetables like courgettes can be planted out. Prepare them for this by hardening off the seedlings (putting them outside during the day for a while) before planting them out; a cold frame does the job, too. This hardening-off process prevents them from going into shock when they are planted, which would stop growth.

You can, of course, plant the seeds straight into the ground outside in May; they will be a little later to fruit, but, not having been moved, they may be sturdier. It's always tempting to plant out as many seedlings as possible, but courgettes take up a lot of space and quite quickly turn into marrows if not picked. They will then slow their production, so it is better to have fewer plants and pick more often.

The lengthened days and sunny weather provide the perfect growing conditions for vegetables. Everything is burgeoning and there is a wealth of fresh produce to eat. Salad leaves can now be sown directly outside – a new row every three weeks or so. In warm, wet weather they can bolt and go to seed in just a few days. Once that has happened, they taste bitter, so it is good to have a succession of planting in case this happens.

Summer vegetables that I enjoy growing are beetroot, fennel, kale and celery. In the greenhouse I will have tomatoes, cucumbers and basil and also a couple of aubergines, although they can be a bit hit-and-miss in the British weather. I always regard growing vegetables as an experiment –sometimes it works and sometimes it doesn't. I try not to be too disappointed when it doesn't and see it as all part of the gardening adventure.

Left: Tomatoes from the white greenhouse. I like to grow a variety of colours for the prettiest of salads. All the sizes, too, from the cherry 'Sungold', to the plum 'Green Envy' and beefsteak 'Brandywine' and 'Costoluto Fiorentino'.

Above: Picking courgettes when they are small encourages more to form, whereas letting them grow too large reduces the plant's productivity.

growing herbs in pots

Over the years I have grown herbs in beds as part of the vegetable patch, but now I prefer to grow them in pots. When you are cooking and you need a sprig of rosemary or a couple of leaves of sage, you really don't want to go any distance to get them. Directly outside the kitchen door is where I grow my herbs, within very easy reaching distance.

Some herbs are a bit thuggish anyway and so are suited to pot growing – like mint, which can take over an entire border within a couple of years and should only ever be grown in a pot. Otherwise, the Mediterranean nature of many herbs makes them suitable for pot growing anyway, keeping their roots on the dry side. Another advantage of this is that they can be moved inside the greenhouse for protection in winter. After a couple of very cold winters when I lost my rosemary both times to lows of –12°C (10°F), I decided I could no longer grow it in the ground.

I use a combination of terracotta and vintage galvanized pots – large ones for spreaders like mint and smaller ones for something like chives. The only herbs I grow in the vegetable patch are parsley, because we eat so much of it, and coriander, because it goes to seed fairly quickly and needs to be resown often. I grow basil in the greenhouse at the start of summer at least, as it enjoys the extra warmth in there.

The herbs I regularly grow are parsley, coriander and basil, which are annuals, and mint, chives, sage, rosemary and oregano, all perennials. Additionally, I grow herb fennel and dill in the gravel garden as I love the look of them there, and they grow too tall for pots.

Above: A pair of sharp snips are useful for cutting rosemary.
Right: A set of steps bought from a vintage store provides a base for herb pots. Placed just outside the kitchen door, they are easy to get to when I need them.

the flower patch in summer

As soon as the risk of frost is over – which is, admittedly, sometimes quite difficult to judge – it's time to plant out the seedlings, and there will be a serious build-up of them waiting to be planted out. It's usually lack of space that forces the first planting session, and fingers are crossed that the nights will be mild from then on.

A couple of rows for each variety will be enough to provide flowers for the house until the first autumn frost. Any extra seedlings can be planted into containers and then placed around the house – a group of pots of different heights flanking a doorway can be attractive and welcoming. I also like to have pots dotted around the eating and sitting areas. Remember to water these well after planting.

In the flower patch, a framework to stop the flowers flopping over is useful. This can be jute netting held in place with bamboo sticks at the corners, although I have to admit I find this a bit hit-and-miss, and liable to collapse under the weight of late-summer foliage. Alternatively, it's possible to make a framework with hazel poles and sticks wired together at crossing points, which has the benefit of lasting a few years. Or simply use bamboo sticks stuck into the ground at intervals to prop up the plants, which can be tied to them with twine. There is a serious eye-poking hazard to this method though, which is why you sometimes see them topped with little upside-down terracotta pots.

The great thing about growing annuals is that once they start blooming, the more you pick the more you get. The plant is always trying to set seed, so if there is a bloom that has gone over, it is important to snip it off – otherwise the plant will think it has done its job and will stop producing flowers. By keeping on top of picking and deadheading, you will have more than enough flowers to grace every flat surface in your house and enough to give away, too. And what could be nicer than arriving at a friend's house with a beautiful hand-tied bouquet of home-grown blooms?

Right: The flower patch is a glorious tumble of blooms by midsummer. A row of sunflowers at the back stands sentinel, in front of which *Ammi majus* provides a froth of white. Beyond that can be seen the yellow spikes of crown daisies, which are so useful for arrangements.

summer flower table

The spring bulbs are over and it's time to plant up a summer display for our table. This will be a shifting party, where seeds that were planted in March will come into bloom and be moved to the table. It's a long season from May to October, so there will be changes along the way.

I start with a couple of ferns; it's always good to have greenery to provide a contrast to flowers and I love the structural shapes they provide. The grey-green *Athyrium niponicum* is a favourite. Added to these are a few bedding plants that I buy each year, usually *Anthemis tinctoria*, the bedding daisy – a summer stalwart – along with bacopa with its tiny white flowers. I also like the bedding form of verbena, which is easy to grow from seed. It not only comes in the traditional bright colours, which I avoid, but also apricot and pale lime greens. If you remember to deadhead them, they will repeat-flower, bringing joy all through the entire growing season.

To these I add small pots of *Erigeron karvinskianus*, which does equally well in pots as in the ground. It self-seeds all around the garden, so is easy to dig up and transplant to a pot. Sown in March, white 'Swan River' daisies provide a cloud of blooms tumbling over the sides of pots. Pots of cosmos, usually on the ground, have big blousy blooms from midsummer onwards. Finally, perhaps, an annual forget-me-not to inject a shot of blue – I like both Chinese and Jamaican. You can add succulents, too: an aeonium at the back to give height and a few smaller ones at the front to provide contrasting shapes. It's all about creating an abundant look – all of summer is here. Yes, it requires water to keep it fresh, but in the hot summers that we are perhaps more likely to get, the garden can be distilled to this one table. Even in the smallest space it is possible to have a bloom-filled table to bring a smile to your face every time you step out. In fact a balcony could be the perfect home for such a display, too.

Left and above: A multitude of pots – all different shapes and sizes – provides an interesting display on the summer flower table. Most of these flowers I have grown from seed, propagated (as with the *Erigeron)* or simply pulled up from the gravel as a young plant and placed in a pot of compost. The succulents and a couple of bedding plants are the only things shown here that I have bought.

using shelves in the garden

Shelves aren't just for books! I love using them in the garden, too. Against a wall at the back of a table they provide not only space for more plants but also vertical interest. Rather in the way that you would have your tallest plants at the back of the border, sets of shelves that are at different heights give the eye something to rest upon.

Auricula theatres – in which auriculas, a beautiful form of primula, are displayed in terracotta pots on shelving, often painted in dark colours to bring out the plants' colours – have been part of the spring garden since the 17th century, but there is so much more use for shelves than this. Succulents look particularly good displayed in this way, but small pots of bedding plants and daisies are also effective.

I'm always on the lookout for interesting shelves, especially with a natural patina. I do sometimes paint them, though. The olive-green set on the facing page, for example, goes very well with the flower colours that I like; a dark paint provides a better background for plants and helps to show them off. A dark burgundy or brown would work equally well. Different shapes of pots can also add interest; as always, anything with patina catches my eye. These are often found in boxes at car boot sales – much the best place to source them, as they can come with quite eye-boggling prices at antique markets, which I suppose just goes to show how sought-after something with genuine age is. There are all sorts of methods available online for aging modern pots, very handy if you want to do that, but nothing is quite as good as the feel and shape of a genuinely old pot. As with everything, slowly building up a collection is the most cost-effective way, or it feels that way at least!

Left: White pelargoniums, *Bacopa* and the tiny 'Swan River' daisy are shelved behind a couple of pots of *Erigeron* cuttings. **Above:** Succulents can withstand the heat of a sunny wall and provide a pretty contrast to the flowers below.

a hand-tied bouquet for a friend

Creating a bouquet for a friend isn't about formal floristry skills, but about showing someone that you love them and have thought about them, and taken the time to create something specially for them. The scent alone will be enough to delight, and a slightly wild bunch of blooms is all the better for not being perfect.

1 Early morning is the best time to pick flowers. Using snips or sharp secateurs, select a mixture of blooms and foliage and cut long stems. Place them in a bucket of water to condition them for at least two hours and up to a day.

2 When you are ready to make your bouquet, strip the leaves from the bottom half of each stem, then lay them all out in easy reach. Cut a long length of twine ready to tie up the finished arrangement.

3 Adding one stem at a time, hold the arrangement loosely in one hand and create a spiral effect by turning it a quarter turn every time you add a stem. You want to have different heights in your bouquet for an informal look, and it's nice to have a couple of bits draping down at the sides, too.

4 When you are happy with your bouquet, tie it securely with the twine, just above your hand.

5 Snip the stems about 5cm (2in) below your hand, straight across so that they are level.

6 You can wrap your flowers in brown paper or tissue paper and tie with a ribbon, or simply present them as they are, ready to be placed in a vase of water.

a natural-looking vase of flowers

You can never have too many vases – that's my story and I'm sticking to it! I have a selection of my mother's vases, which I cherish, but I also enjoy picking them up in junk shops and thrift stores. A simple shape – either tapering slightly or straight up – and in subtle, mostly natural colours, will suit a relaxed arrangement. Simplicity is what it's about and often the humble jam jar will work perfectly.

Although I am creating a very relaxed look, balance is still important. This can be achieved with a range of textures and forms to provide visual contrast. Limiting the range of colours helps to create a cohesive look, and I often like to include some green. There are no hard-and-fast rules here, but it is helpful to keep the size of vase and the size of arrangement in balance. A very tall arrangement in a short vase just looks a little odd, as does a very wide one in a thin vase. Confusingly, however, this does not apply to bowls, which can accommodate both tall and wide arrangements and look fine. But bowls do give a slightly more formal, 'arranged' look, which is why I mostly stick to vases. The best thing is to experiment and see what suits you.

Using a flower frog can help keep your stems in the position in which you place them, but for a more relaxed look I prefer a piece of chicken wire scrunched up into a ball. Before placing the stem in the vase, make a diagonal cut at the base to maximize water absorption. I would suggest limiting your flower varieties to three or five, as it is better to have a few stems of the same flower than one each of several different species. For contrast, use different textures: for example, *Ammi majus*, which is airy and light, mixed with more solid cosmos creates a nice balance. Having just one variety can also look wonderful and is very simple to achieve: for example, a large, eye-catching jug of ox-eye daisies.

Left: Using just one type of flower can be very effective, as with these pretty cosmos. A mix of blooms (above) is more flamboyant and colourful.

Overleaf: A range of vessels, from an urn and an old jelly mould to a simple glass jar, each give a different feeling to an arrangement, from sweetly simple to dramatic abundance.

pressed-flower picture

There is something so nostalgic about pressing flowers – the whole process is rich in childhood memories. I began by pressing flowers and leaves between two newspaper pages, which were then placed under the corner of the heavy rug in our sitting room. Then, one birthday, I was given a flower press, and the process of winding and unwinding the wingnuts became an enjoyable part of the procedure, leading up to the big reveal of the newly dried blooms. Sometimes I made a collage to present to my mother, as if handing her an Oscar.

1 For the best effect, choose flowers that are not quite in full bloom. Pick them in the morning, after any dew has dried, because damp flowers will go mouldy. For large flowers, it's best to separate the petals and then reconstruct them as you stick them to your paper. In fact, I prefer pressing smaller flowers, like daisies and cow parsley, which create an airy, delicate look when dried.

2 A flower press will give the most reliable results. Start off by laying the flowers on sheets of blotting paper. To create an even press, arrange flowers of similar thickness on each sheet of blotting paper. Place the flower heads face-down on the paper with enough space between them so that they are not touching – putting them face-down will make them less likely to move and get crumpled when you sandwich the layers together.

3 Place another piece of blotting paper over the flowers, then a piece of thick card on top, before another piece of blotting paper begins the next layer. Continue in this way until you have completed your layers, then place the wooden top on the flower press and tighten the wing nuts.

Above: Dried flowers are delicate. Craft tweezers with sharp points are the best way of handling them in order to minimize damage to the brittle stems.

4 Over the following days, tighten the nuts a few times, as the flowers begin to dry out. Then it's just a matter of waiting for three weeks, the hardest part, until the pressed flowers are ready to be made into pictures.

5 To create a picture, you will need paper that is good for mounting, such as parchment or watercolour paper. I like an antique look so I choose gentle, slightly faded colours, such as ivory or stone. The slightly flecked effect from Lokta paper looks good, too. Whatever you use, it should be acid free. You will also need a matte craft glue like Mod Podge, a small paintbrush, a craft knife for cutting stems and a pair of sharp tweezers for the delicate job of moving your dried pieces around. Using tweezers, carefully remove your flowers from the press and arrange them on the mounting paper. Finalize your design before beginning to glue. Once you are happy with how it looks, you can begin sticking.

6 Glue each piece in place, making sure every part of the flower is attached to the paper. Now gently brush glue over it all, to seal everything. This will dry to become invisible quite quickly. After a few hours it will be ready to frame.

Above: A sturdily made flower press like this one, with a plywood top and bottom, will provide an even pressure on to the flowers without any risk of the top bending as the wingnuts are tightened.

sourcing vintage picture frames

I'm always on the lookout for old photo frames, which give my pressed-flower pictures a vintage look in keeping with the tones of the flowers. I prefer to use something that isn't shiny and perfect but has had the odd knock. Charity shops are a very good hunting ground for these, as the frames get cleared out of homes – unwanted to some, they are exactly what I am looking for.

Online auctions are also worth a look – remember, however, that a frame without glass may appear a bargain, but getting glass cut is a faff and adds to the price. I prefer plain wooden frames, without any gold – the plainer the better, in fact. Steer away from that orange pine and towards dark-brown wood, unvarnished if possible. A small plain oak frame will set off a simple pressed-flower design perfectly.

If the frame is looking a little shiny, it's possible to tone this down with varnish remover. Take out the backing and the glass and carefully paint on the remover using an old brush, leaving this as long as the instructions on the tin indicate. It is then usually possible to wipe off the varnish, perhaps using wire wool if it is a little stubborn. After cleaning with a damp cloth to remove all traces of the treatment, you can leave it in its plain unvarnished state or polish with beeswax and a soft cloth to achieve a gentle sheen.

Alternatively, a coat of chalk paint can transform a more modern frame and needs the minimum of preparation before application. If you add a layer of a contrasting colour first, a vintage effect can be achieved with a light sand to reveal the base colour.

Left: A simple design of dill flowers and daisies is set off by a prettily carved frame – one of my favourite finds.
Above: A selection of frames that I have found, including one from a French *brocante*, or flea market.

an outdoor space for relaxing

Summer isn't all about doing – it is also about being. With so much of the gardening hard work having been done in spring, it's important to allow ourselves to stop and appreciate that hard work, and actually enjoy being in the space we have created. Making an inviting area in which to relax is a way of encouraging ourselves to slow down a little and make the most of the season.

At some point in May, usually at the first spell of warm, sunny weather, it is time for me to dust off three rattan sofas and to make space for them by moving the small table and chairs that have stood on the kitchen terrace all winter. I bring cushions out of storage and replant my big galvanized pots with cosmos. This is the moment that summer begins for me, and from now on I will try to spend as much time as possible outside. Of course, the vagaries of British weather mean that this isn't always possible, but I'd rather be in the greenhouse listening to the patter of rain on the roof while I pot up my seedlings than be inside the house.

A rug or throw placed under a tree is a good place to start with this serious relaxation. It's important to have shade, because sitting in bright sunlight can make us overheat quickly and glare can make reading impossible. If there is no satisfactory tree, a parasol will do. When erecting it on a patch of lawn, it is a good idea to sink a section of metal tubing into the ground that the parasol will sit in. The top of the tube should be just below the level of the ground so as not to catch in the lawn mower. Doing this means that you will not be shifting a very heavy base on and off the lawn every week. Once you've found your spot, lay out a couple of picnic blankets or throws, or even a threadbare rug. Add a comfortable chair or just a few cushions. Faded vintage fabrics give a relaxed romantic feel and a nice ambience. A low stool or a tray is good for putting a jug and glasses on. I love threading solar lights around the branches of a tree – they look so pretty as dusk falls. Battery-powered fairy lights wound around a parasol look good, too.

If you don't have a lot of shade in your garden, you may want to invest in a gazebo or a bell tent, to create an outdoor living area. A website such as eBay is a good place to look for second-hand large canvas awnings and tents – in my mind highly preferable to the flimsy plastic gazebos available new. A sail awning is another option, with perhaps one corner tied to a tree and two poles at the others. Whatever you use, the aim is to create an inviting, relaxing space to while away warm afternoons in reading, listening to a podcast, soaking up the sounds of summer or just drifting off.

Left: An old lounger, originally from India, has found a summer resting spot under a quince tree. The fabric for the cushions was recycled from some old curtains and I made the bunting out of scraps of leftover fabric.

a simple way to update cushions

A quick way to refresh and update your seating area is to make new covers for outdoor dining chairs. I like pads on outdoor chairs for comfort, but they occasionally get left out in the rain and start to look a bit untidy, while still being serviceable. A very simple new cover will completely revive them. I like to use a mix of fabrics for an eclectic look, but with a connecting theme. I'm a bit of a fabric hoarder, keeping leftover scraps for years until I find a purpose for them. Furnishing fabric works best here for durability but I have also used dressmaking material. A fabric warehouse or a store that sells ends of rolls is a great place to search for small, inexpensive cut-offs, as are market stalls.

1 Cut out a piece of fabric the width of your cushion plus 10cm (4in), and twice the length of the cushion plus 20cm (8in). For example, if your cushion is 40cm (16in) square, your fabric piece should be 50cm (20in) wide by 100cm (40in) long.

2 Press a 5mm (¼in) hem to the wrong side on each of the two short edges; stitch.

3 Lay out the fabric, right side up, and place the cushion on top, in the middle. Fold in the hemmed ends snugly so they overlap in the centre of the cushion cover.

With the raw edges even, pin a seam along one side, with the pins in a line close to the cushion. Remove the cushion and stitch the pinned seam, taking out the pins as you go.

4 With the cover still wrong side out, insert the cushion between the two layers and pin the remaining seam as before, so the fabric fits snugly. Remove the cushion via the opening and stitch the pinned seam as in step 3. Press the seams, turn the cover right side out, press again and insert the cushion.

Above: A shady spot under a tree provides the perfect escape from the summer sun.
Right: Seat cushions with their new covers.

a summer table

Is there anything better than a long summer evening spent outside, sitting with friends, soft music playing in the background, the air still warm from the day? As dusk falls, I know I would rather be in my own garden than anywhere else in the world.

In reality, how many evenings a year does that happen? Probably a handful at most, which makes them all the more special. Generally, however, it is safer to have some sort of protection in the form of a porch, greenhouse or gazebo, with the added bonus that candles are less likely to be blown out by the breeze.

A simple outdoor supper with the smallest posy of flowers on the table can be delightful, but every now and again something more celebratory is needed. There's so much abundance in the garden right now that it doesn't feel too extravagant to pick an armful of flowers – it's a useful form of deadheading anyhow! A nice idea is to provide every diner with their own tied posy that can be taken home at the end of the evening. A selection of small vases or jam jars is all that's needed for this. There are really no rules, either – the flowers can be as simple or as extravagant as you like, although height is a factor; it's no good sitting with a gorgeous bunch of flowers in front of you which is also blocking your view of the person opposite.

A muted palette can look smart and elegant, and a colourful one exuberant and joyful, but the individual posies do need to connect to each other in colour and size. They can be tied up simply with either twine or ribbon. Tea lights dotted around the table complete the look.

Above and right: The joy of outdoor eating. Small jars of flowers dotted around the table can look enchanting. Posies tied with a piece of ribbon can easily be lifted and taken home by your guests as mementoes.

Flower-filled jam jars hanging from tree branches look very romantic and pretty. You can tie garden twine or thin wire around the neck of each jar to create a hanging loop. Having jars at different levels looks best but don't hang them so low that they hit the guests' heads or obscure the view across the table. Fill the jars with a few blooms each – hanging tendrils can look very effective. Dark colours will be less visible as the evening darkens, whereas light colours, especially white, will glow. Battery-operated or solar-powered fairy lights will add to the magical atmosphere.

creating a kitchen with personality

A large proportion of our time is spent in this important room, so why not make it more than a clinical workspace? The heart of the home should appeal to the hearts of its occupants and reflect their personalities. By making small changes this can be achieved very simply.

Kitchens have come so far from the original modern design, which was all about function and labour-saving efficiency, with easy-to-clean surfaces and identikit units. Fashions change in all decorating areas, including kitchens, so it's helpful to have good basic elements that are adaptable. Quality carcasses are worth investing in, being strongly made; they will last the test of time. New doors and hardware can be added, or just a different paint colour, which can change the mood of the kitchen completely. The worktop is the other important element, and worth spending more on at the beginning. Our worktop is silestone, made from a mixture of natural minerals and recycled materials, which is non-porous and extremely durable.

When we first moved here, the kitchen was one of our major renovations. We extended it by about a metre (3 feet), adding French windows leading out to the terrace. We also knocked through to the pantry at the other end of the room, where my mother had done the washing-up out of sight. It had been such a dark room during my childhood that I wanted it to be bright and light, so I chose light-coloured cabinets and off-white walls with white tiling. However, after ten years I was ready for a complete change. The original Neptune kitchen was still in perfectly good order, so with the help of a local joiner we made small changes, such as reversing the doors for a plainer look and swapping the tiles for matchboard. By making a floor-to-ceiling larder cupboard from the original fridge-freezer surround, we created a totally new look. Painting the units black completed the dramatic look I was after – it feels much more 'me' than my previous, pale kitchen.

Using wallpaper was a choice that I haven't regretted for a minute. It did take me a long time to choose the right one – 'Under the Elder Tree' from Boråstapeter – as it can be quite daunting picking a design, especially as it's not a small investment. Wallpaper certainly is a great way of injecting personality into a kitchen, however.

Other new touches include a vintage cabinet for glasses fitted at the end of the wide shelf behind the Aga, complemented by a shelf unit on the worktop at the other end for my collection of studio pottery mugs. I love the mix of practical units with vintage pieces, as it turns the space into something unique and individual.

Right: A row of units along one side of the kitchen. The shelf above is supported by metal prongs. which were inserted and plastered into the wall so that the shelf would be strong enough to support crockery.

Overleaf, left: A shelving unit displays a collection of pottery mugs; a sleeping cat in her English-made willow basket; the view through to the hallway; and upcycling a vintage wooden magazine rack as a holder for chopping boards.

Overleaf right: A cupboard bought on eBay holds everyday pieces: glasses for drinking water and cups for the coffee machine below. The bread bin sits next to the toaster; having things in easy reach is always helpful.

summer recipes

They say growing your own vegetables is a case of feast or famine, and, happily, summer is all about feasting. Even if you don't have your own veg patch, food shops are full of fresh, locally grown produce, and a weekly local market is a great place to pick up an abundance of reasonably priced produce.

roasted tomato sauce

If you are growing vegetables – and even if you are not – the freezer is your friend in the summer months. I make large batches of tomato sauce, using some on the day and freezing the rest. Adding a touch of summer to a meal on a cold winter's evening can make such a difference. Roasting the garlic in its skin creates a smooth, sweet, aromatic clove and prevents it from burning. The natural use for this is, of course, pasta, as it really elevates this simple dish into something memorable. It's also great as a pizza topping – you could reduce it a little first to thicken it. I also use it as a base for curry sauce and, in fact, anything else that calls for a tin of tomatoes.

Makes 1–1.5 litres

2kg (4lb 8oz) ripe tomatoes, or enough to fill a large roasting tin

3 garlic cloves, unpeeled

2 rosemary sprigs

1 red chilli (optional)

about 3 tablespoons olive oil

1 tablespoon sea salt flakes

pepper

Preheat the oven to 200°C (400°F), Gas Mark 6.

Cut each tomato through its equator and place face-up in a large roasting tray. Add the garlic cloves, rosemary sprigs and chilli, if using, then drizzle with the olive oil and season well with the salt and pepper. Roast the tomatoes for about 50 minutes, or until the edges are just beginning to caramelize. This will add lots of flavour. Remove from the oven and allow to cool.

Slip the garlic cloves out of their skins and pull the rosemary leaves from their stalks. Place everything in a blender and liquidize to a smooth consistency. This may take a while, but it's worth the extra time to get a really glossy, velvety sauce. Freeze in batches, enough for one meal each.

pickled chillies

Chillies are so easy to grow, whether in pots in the greenhouse or on a sunny windowsill. I'm always a little over-enthusiastic in spring and I end up with multiple varieties – pots groaning with chillies come midsummer, so this recipe is a delicious way of preserving them. It also makes them sweeter and more mellow, dialling down the heat, which can be helpful for particularly ferocious varieties.

To fill a 475ml (17fl oz) jar

- 500g (1lb 2oz) chillies (any variety)
- 2 fresh bay leaves
- 120ml (4¼fl oz) cider vinegar
- 120ml (4¼fl oz) water
- 65g (2¼oz) caster sugar
- 1 tablespoon mustard seeds
- 1 tablespoon coriander seeds
- 2 teaspoons salt

After trimming the stalks, slice the chillies thinly – there's no need to remove the seeds. It's a good idea to wear protective gloves for this task, to prevent a few hours of burning fingers! Place the chillies in a sterilized 475ml (17fl oz) airtight jar (see page 185), then slide the bay leaves down the inside of the jar.

Put all the remaining ingredients in a small saucepan on a medium heat, stirring occasionally until the sugar has dissolved. Bring to the boil, then carefully pour the liquid over the chillies. Seal the jar with the lid, using a cloth to protect yourself from the heat, and allow to cool to room temperature. Store in the refrigerator for 3 weeks before using; they will keep for up to 6 months if stored in a cool, dark cupboard.

quick pickled onions

An easy, all-year-round way of making a transformative topping for hot and cold salads, bread and cheese, risotto, eggs on toast and much more, these pickled onions improve almost any meal.

To fill a 350ml (12fl oz) jar

- 2 red onions
- 2 teaspoons caster sugar
- 1 teaspoon sea salt
- 1 teaspoon sumac
- 1 tablespoon red wine vinegar

Peel and cut the onions in half, then slice very thinly and place in a bowl. Add all the other ingredients and mix well, separating the layers of onion as you are stirring. Leave for at least 1 hour, although 3 is better. Place in a clean 350ml (12fl oz) airtight jar and seal with the lid. Keep in the refrigerator and use within 2 weeks.

lime and polenta cake

The zing of lime is such a summertime association for me. This is summer in cake form. Perfect for eating outside under the shade of a tree, it also works well as a pudding served with a spoonful of crème fraîche. The polenta makes it slightly more fragile than cake made with flour, and it needs handling with care once baked, but the flavour is wonderful.

Serves 8

- 200g (7oz) butter at room temperature, plus extra for greasing
- 200g (7oz) caster sugar
- 3 large eggs
- 200g (7oz) ground almonds
- grated zest and juice of 2 limes, zest reserved for the syrup
- 100g (3½oz) fine polenta
- 1 teaspoon baking powder
- 80g (3oz) shelled pistachio nuts

For the syrup

- 100g (3½oz) caster sugar
- 100ml (3½fl oz) water
- reserved lime zest (see above)

Preheat the oven to 180°C (350°F), Gas Mark 4. Grease a 23cm (9in) round springform cake tin.

Zest the limes into a small saucepan for the syrup.

Beat the butter and caster sugar together in a stand mixer, or with a wooden spoon in a large mixing bowl, until pale and fluffy. Add the eggs, one at a time, and beat until fully incorporated. Gently mix in the ground almonds, with the mixer on a low speed if using. Add the lime juice and then carefully mix in the polenta along with the baking powder.

Scrape the cake batter into the tin and bake for 30–40 minutes, or until a sharp knife inserted into the cake comes out clean.

While the cake is baking, heat the ingredients for the syrup in a small saucepan and boil for 2 minutes, stirring. Set aside.

When the cake is ready, remove from the oven and allow to cool for a few minutes in the tin on a wire rack.

Prick the top of the cake all over with a cocktail stick and pour over the syrup, allowing it to soak in. Spread the pistachios out on a baking sheet and toast in the oven for 5 minutes, then remove and allow to cool before roughly chopping. When the cake is completely cool, run a sharp knife around the edge of the tin before carefully removing the cake from the tin. Sprinkle the chopped pistachios over the top.

a cake decorated with fresh flowers

Decorating a cake with fresh flowers can make a beautiful dessert or a very special afternoon tea. I always make a standard Victoria sponge for this, with jam sandwiching the layers and vanilla frosting to cover the cake. It's best to use plain frosting so that the flowers stand out against it but you could use a pastel food colouring, too.

There is a huge range of edible flowers in summer, and tendrils of thyme can look and taste lovely with the flowers. Among a long list of edibles are violets and pansies, nasturtiums (flowers and leaves), borage, calendula (marigold), cornflower, elderflower and daisy. I picked these from my own garden, but online suppliers also provide a range of (pesticide-free) wildflowers.

It's a good idea to use flowers that are roughly the same size for an even effect. It does have to be done at the last minute, onto fresh frosting. The flowers won't stay perfect-looking for very long, so if you need to have something that will keep, it's better to use pressed flowers, which give a slightly different look but are very effective. I have used this method for decorating a wedding cake. It requires more forethought as the blooms need to be pressed for three weeks to dry. Whichever flowers you use, place them around the edge of the cake, pressing them gently into the frosting. It looks good if you have several different heights of stem, some of which stand up above the top of the cake, so that when you have finished about a third of the blooms stick up over the cake, which looks so pretty.

Right: A mixture of herbs and edible flowers can be used to elevate a humble Victoria sponge; it becomes a fitting part of a memorable occasion.

autumn

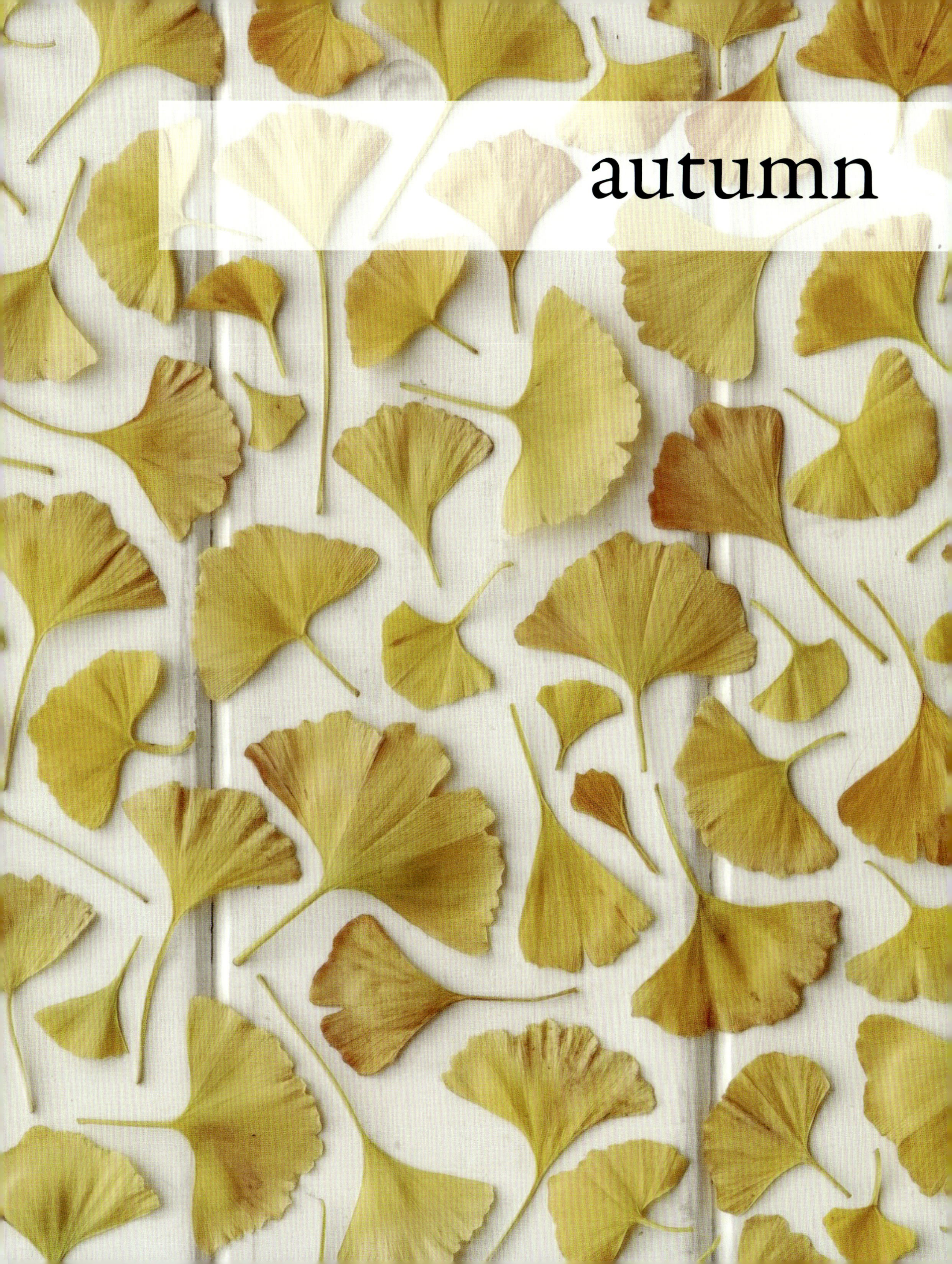

Every year, at some point in early September, I become aware of a change in the light. It seems softer somehow – the harsh vertical rays of high summer are gone, replaced by a hazy warmth that can occasionally still become proper heat, but without the intensity of previous months. There's a laziness about the insects buzzing around, and their slowing activity is mirrored by the plants, which have reached their zenith. The greens of summer are becoming tawny golds and warm browns. As everything slackens outside, the desire to be cosy increases. The year is beginning its gentle wind down – autumn has arrived.

As the final harvest in the fields signals the end of the growing season, there are fewer tasks in the garden, but so much to enjoy: watching the leaves turn golden and then fall, the slow retreat indoors to find a cosy corner to sit and read. Then, in the kitchen, cooking soups that nourish and prepare us for the cooler months ahead. Leaning into autumn gives us plenty to relish.

Right: The shortening periods of daylight mean meals lit by candles, golden afternoons and golden leaves. The vines in the greenhouse begin their fall into slumber and I welcome the cosy glow of a candle when I take a moment's rest.

the vegetable patch in autumn

It's such a wonderful autumn sight to see: pumpkins and squash displayed on a table in the sunshine – a sign that all your hard work has created produce that will feed you during the cold months ahead.

The squash that were tiny seedlings back in April now roam wildly, their tendrils reaching up to 3–4.5 metres (10–15 feet). Peel back the leaves and you discover several fattening butternut squash that you hadn't noticed. The fruit need all the available sunshine now, so removing the largest leaves is a good idea. When they are no longer growing and are ready to harvest, cut them off, leaving a generous amount of stalk that will enable them to be stored for longer. They will enjoy a sunbathe on a table or bench for a few days to harden their skin ready for storing.

Continue to pick courgettes to keep them producing until the first hard frost, when they will quietly fold into themselves and shrink down very quickly. Beetroot, spinach and carrots are familiar ingredients on our supper plates at this time of year, but these won't be affected by the frost. In fact, my mother always told me not to pick leeks until after a frost as it improved their flavour.

Successional sowing of salad leaves is still important, to ensure a supply of salad through the winter. Some are suitable for growing outside, like land cress, which I have found to be great for filling the hunger gap the following March. There are winter salad mixes available that are more resilient to cold weather. I also grow salad in the greenhouse in old animal troughs and in the beds when the tomato plants have been removed. This way we can have a handful of green for our lunch every day throughout the winter, without the need to buy one of those exorbitantly priced bags filled with noxious gases and limp bits of salad leaf.

Left: Leaving pumpkins on a sunny table for a couple of weeks will allow their skins to harden, ready for storage.
Above: Chard sown in late summer is a valuable vegetable in the colder months, when other leaves are sparse.

Autumn brings bounty, not only of vegetables but also of fruit. Apples and pears, which grow so abundantly in the UK climate, are ready to be picked. Is there anything better than the first apple crumble of the season? If you don't have access to a cooking-apple tree, buy British apples and pears, which are readily available. Right: Ripening quince, which add a fragrant piquancy to sweet and savoury dishes.

the autumn flower patch

Dahlias are the stars of the season. I like to grow a selection of softer, warmer colours that suit autumn, rather than the bright pinks that look good in August but somehow seem out of place with the warm tones that are everywhere later in the year.

You can buy plants that are already flowering from midsummer onwards, which is useful if you want to be sure of the colour you are getting. However, it does make it more expensive. Dahlias can also be grown from seed, but the easiest way is to buy tubers. I remember a plantsman telling me once that the best time to buy dahlias is Valentine's Day, which struck me as a very satisfactory activity on that particular day. Tubers are available from late January to May. Planting them early into pots gives you a head start, but they do need to be protected from frost at this stage, and it's essential not to overwater them as they are liable to rot. They can be planted out after the last frost in late May or June, by which time they should have some healthy-looking shoots.

Dahlias are irresistible to slugs, and it can be devastating to come upon the plants the following day to find only a few short nubs left. I have found that copper rings work well as a deterrent. Place them at the base, wedging them slightly into the ground so that the slugs can't get in through any gaps. Once the dahlias have got established and the lower shoots have toughened up, they become less attractive to the dreaded invasion and go on to produce their glorious blooms from mid-July until the first frost.

I grow all of my dahlias in the fenced-in flower patch. It's partly to protect them from deer, but also I think dahlias grow better all together here than in a border, where they somehow don't look their best to me, mixed in with other perennials. They are also much easier to pick in the flower patch, as I don't have to clamber over other plants (and they do need regular picking and deadheading to prolong the production of flowers). I tend not to lift my dahlias at the end of the season – they have to manage through the winter outside, albeit

Left: Some favourite dahlias: yellow 'Bishop of York', caramel-coloured 'David Howard' and, behind that, the dark tones of 'Verrone's Obsidian' and the pure-white 'My Love'. **Above:** 'Honka Yellow' shining like stars in the dahlia patch.

under a thick mulch. They are actually much hardier than we think – mine have, on occasions, survived –14°C (7°F).

Some of my favourite dahlia varieties are 'My Love', 'Honka Fragile', 'Sweet Nathalie', 'Café au Lait' (all of these paler shades), and, among the warmer colours, 'Sylvia', 'Bishop of York', 'David Howard' and 'Verrone's Obsidian'.

Other flowers that come into their own in autumn include rudbeckia, with its lovely warm colours. I especially like *Rudbeckia hirta*, which also grows well in containers and is a useful perennial. Amaranthus is such a theatrical and fun annual to grow from seed, and really adds drama to an arrangement, a bit like adding a woolly scarf to a vase of flowers. I particularly love the fresh green and copper varieties.

Above: Dahlia 'David Howard'.
Right: An autumn vase comprising yellow rudbeckia, bronze fennel, wild carrot and *Stipa gigantea*. The now-drying grasses complement the soft colours of the season perfectly.

The soft tones of sunflowers are also synonymous with autumn for me. It is no longer just the bright yellow that fills fields so joyfully – there is a huge selection of colours available. Finally, that summer staple, cosmos are still flowering their socks off, not just the white of summer but also yellows and oranges for autumn. The more you pick, the more you get – every surface may have a jam jar filled with them, making the most of every bloom until the first hard frost, when their season comes to an abrupt end.

Collecting seeds to store over winter for spring sowing is a great way of saving money. I love to think that several generations of a plant are growing in my garden, in a continuation of the rhythm of life that makes me happy.

bulb ordering

Now is the time to start thinking about spring bulbs, just as the garden is winding down. It's always good to have something to look forward to next year, and a sit-down with a bulb catalogue and a cup of tea is a very pleasant way to spend a rainy autumn afternoon, especially if there is cake involved.

Narcissi, including prepared paperwhites for indoor flowering, are the first to choose, then daffodils, hyacinths, muscari and, finally, tulips. With so much choice, a lot of money can be spent in a short space of time! A way of keeping things reasonable is to pick a restricted colour scheme and stick to it, rather than allowing yourself to be attracted by all the different colours, of tulips in particular. I always go for whites and yellows to align with the narcissi and then apricots and soft oranges. Something on the aubergine spectrum always seems to creep in, too, but it does provide a good contrast with the paler colours.

In the following weeks a series of small cardboard boxes arrive, some a complete surprise, as I have already forgotten my fever of ordering. They need to be stored somewhere dry and as dark as possible, until you are ready to plant. Daffodils should be in the ground by the end of October to give them time to develop roots before winter. Tulips can go in much later, up to Christmas and even January; planting at this time reduces the risk of fungal disease.

Left: A long-handled bulb planter minimizes back strain, and allows you to apply more downward force to hard ground.
Above: In borders where the ground is softer, a long narrow trowel does the job.

autumn flower arranging

There's something theatrical about dahlias, so they need to be displayed in a way that suits their dramatic personality. No small posy for them – it's best to go big with your dahlias, which is also a good way of celebrating what is almost the end of the cut flower season.

An urn or a large jug is a good vessel for displaying dahlias. Seedheads are in abundance right now, providing contrast to the solid shapes of the flowers. Grasses, too, are thriving, and adding a bough of amber leaves – from a maple, for example – can look stunning. Opulence is what you are going for, as it's a celebratory moment: the culmination of the growing season and the bounty of the garden. Placing a couple of apples, or even a small pumpkin or two, at the base of your arrangement can be a nice seasonal touch.

Like daffodils, dahlias can look effective displayed in tall bottles – a collection of five bottles with the addition of some rudbeckia and fennel flowers will look stunning, especially against a dark wall, which will complement their strong colours. It's such a simple way of creating something eye-catching, and it can be done in minutes.

A windowsill is a good way to display these, too, the light shining through translucent petals a beautiful way of showing off the flowers. I also like that this can be a visual diary of what I've grown in a certain year, particularly with daffodils; it acts as an aide memoire for future years, so don't just display your bulbs, remember to photograph them, too.

Above and right: Two different styles of urn complement the drama of autumn flowers. A tendril of amaranthus adds interest in one, while drying hydrangea blooms are included on the right.

Overleaf: Bottles are a good way of showcasing dahlias, mixed here with yellow rudbeckia and bronze fennel. A pretty way of displaying narcissi is to put each different variety in its own bottle.

pumpkin table centrepiece

A fun way of making a table centrepiece is to fill a hollowed-out pumpkin with flowers. A traditional orange one fits the bill, although a slightly softer orange in a flatter shape, usually one of the heirloom varieties, is my favourite. These have the bonus of a flatter bottom, which makes them more stable. Either pale orange or green (like 'Crown Prince') or a warty one works well; you can also make soup or pie from the flesh, so nothing is wasted.

1 With a sharp knife, carefully cut out a lid from the top of the pumpkin and scoop out the flesh and seeds with a spoon. In the cavity, place the largest vessel that will fit in the space – either a jam jar or a bowl shape works well. Fill that with water and add a flower frog.

2 Start with a few short branches of autumn leaves, then add dahlias to give structure in a dome-like shape. Finally, fill in the gaps with smaller blooms or seedheads. It doesn't have to be too neat, but the fact that it will be seen from all angles needs to be taken into account.

an autumn wreath

I think autumn is perhaps my favourite time of year to make a wreath, as there is still so much bounty in the garden in the way of foliage and seedheads. Most of it has begun the drying process while still standing, which means that it will last a fair amount of time once cut. Now is also the time to make wreath rings out of prunings – simple to construct, these can be reused many times.

A wreath ring can be made out of many types of tree or shrub cuttings. Willow, dogwood and birch are all good options. Using the stems from autumn pruning is a very satisfactory form of upcycling. They need to be bendy – anything that is not this year's growth is liable to snap – and a reasonable length. Trim off any side shoots and crisping foliage to leave bare stems. Lay two of the longest stems against each other with the cut ends staggered by about 15cm (6in). Wind them together, twisting both as you go, until you come to the end of the stems. Tuck in the ends tightly between the wound stems so that they are trapped firmly; trim off any excess. Now add extra lengths in the same way, always starting at a different point to give the overall structure strength.

Sometimes it takes a few experiments to find the right material. Vines work well, with their long growth in one year, which provides the right sort of flexibility. Silver birch is easy to weave using several stems at once, and makes a very pretty unadorned wreath just by itself.

Above: A wreath ring made out of the chocolate vine (*Akebia quinata*) which is strong yet very pliable.
Right: The finished wreath, as detailed overleaf.

1 Collect armfuls of material, such as bracken, acer, traveller's joy, and fennel or *Ammi majus* seedheads. I have included some crab-apple berries, as their warm amber colour is a good addition. Grass seedheads can be used, too.

2 Start by cutting lengths of foliage, all slightly different in size – we are not looking for a neat, uniform circle here. Gather three or four pieces together into a bunch, and then wire this bunch of foliage to the wreath ring at an angle slanting to the right. Add more bunches of foliage; I find it easiest to work anticlockwise around the ring, but either direction works. The closer they are together, the more abundant the finished effect will be.

3 When you have covered the entire ring, make a loop in the wire with which to hang up the wreath, and tie in the end of the wire tightly. Hang the wreath on a door, wall or peg rail, indoors or out. It should last for a few weeks, slowly becoming more curly and dried, but none the worse for that.

Above and left: Bracken, traveller's joy, acer, alder, beech and the little yellow crab apple (*Malus sieboldii*) are all used here, providing a joyful abundance.

a decorated pumpkin

Decorating a pumpkin with pressed leaves is an effective way of making a beautiful Halloween display and is really useful if your pumpkin-carving skills aren't at expert level. A collection of three decorated pumpkins looks good on some steps or by a door, or you could use them as part of a tabletop decoration. By this time of year there are plenty of fallen brown leaves to use.

1 At least two or three weeks before you need them, collect some dry leaves and press them (see pages 82–3). Bracken, which grows so plentifully in the UK and is now turning brown, is also suitable. Select pumpkins with a fairly flat base so that they don't roll around once they've been decorated. I like using the creamy white pumpkins, which come in all different sizes and are usually available from farm shops.

2 Choose a medium-sized pumpkin and wipe it clean; make sure the surface is dry. Using a paintbrush, brush a layer of craft adhesive such as Mod Podge over the entire skin. This will dry to a matte finish, creating a good surface on which to stick the leaves.

3 Cover the reverse side of one leaf or bracken frond well with the adhesive and position on the pumpkin. You will need to hold it in place for a while.

4 Repeat step 3 for the other leaves and bracken fronds – adding leaves in a fairly random pattern looks good. You may have to return to a stubborn end of a leaf or piece of bracken to hold it down again. Covering each leaf with more glue will help get them to stick and will provide a tough outer glaze.

the garden studio shed

For a while I had wanted a dedicated and fuss-free space for flower faffing, so I gave my husband the task of building me a studio shed in the orchard. We wanted to repurpose an existing shed rather than build from new, and so the search on eBay began.

It had to be large enough for my needs but transportable once deconstructed, and in a condition good enough to make it worthwhile. We did find the perfect thing, but it was in Scotland – there are limits to the distance Thomas will travel, even for me! Finally, one turned up in Hampshire that was exactly the right size and shape. It had been custom-made for the owner and was therefore of great quality, and available for a fraction of the price that he had paid to have it made. We snapped it up.

After six concrete footings had been laid, the shed slowly began to take shape one spring. A corrugated-tin roof was added and, best of all, a veranda on which to sit with a cup of tea or a book, protected from the weather. I had been inspired by pictures of Australian houses with their verandas, so was thrilled that mine would have one, too. I found windows on Facebook Marketplace, and used a couple of glazed cabinet doors to make two more. Some friends of ours donated the beautiful old floorboards.

I wanted to make the interior look like an old scout hut and so mixed up a wash with watered-down emulsion paint, which I wiped with a cloth to show up the wood grain in the panelling. To store vases and floristry equipment, I co-opted a big old cupboard that we already had. I found a table online and painted it, and all the other bits I have picked up slowly. Nothing is new and everything has sentimental value or appealed to me because of its timeworn look. This room has become much more than a place for photography and flower arranging. We often eat in there, especially in the winter with the wood burner alight. In the summer sun the veranda a lovely place for breakfast. This is the perfect way to greet the day, soaking up the sights and sounds of the season.

Left: I wanted the shed to have a cottage-garden feel. The narrow borders around it are filled with daisies, foxgloves and *Ammi majus*. The bicycle is a permanent fixture, its basket filled with flowers to add a touch of romance.
Above: A perfect place to daydream, sitting on the veranda underneath the vine.

ideas for decorating projects

The shift in the season and the move indoors again can spark a desire for change in our interior surroundings. Whether it is simply altering the layout of furniture to create a cosier atmosphere or swapping cushion covers, after a long summer of outdoor living we suddenly see things with new eyes and feel inspired to make changes.

From making the smallest alteration to redecorating an entire room, there is the traditional deadline of Christmas to spur us on, although why everything has to be done by then, I'm not sure!

You can achieve small but effective changes with textiles. I remember my mother telling me how as a child her own mother would swap the curtains twice a year, having a winter set and a summer one. I love the idea of this, although storing all those curtains would present a bit of a challenge. I do understand the desire for marking the seasons, though, in the same way that the world outside changes from fresh greens to earthy browns between summer and winter. It is nice to echo that by using warmer tones in the home when the cold season approaches. Simply swapping cushion covers could be the small difference needed to embrace the upcoming cooler weather. The selection of fabric is also important – replacing the linens of summer with velvets and thicker, more tactile fabrics is a sensual way of making a seasonal change. Add throws in complementing colours over the backs of sofas to encourage cosy moments in the day. A pile of books or magazines can entice us to sit down and dream, if only for a while.

Switching around pictures can also alter the look of a room. Or you may wish to add to your collection. By using an old frame with an inexpensive print you can create a look that doesn't cost the earth. I've also made my own frames from wooden moulding, available quite cheaply from hardware stores. It does help to have a mitring tool to make neat corners, but it's not essential. Two coats of chalk paint in contrasting colours reveal a vintage effect when the top layer is lightly sanded; the frame can then be waxed and buffed to a soft sheen.

Right: An old French cupboard is home to all my fabric remnants. I never throw anything away; even the smallest scrap can be used to make bunting, or for quilting. Some pieces sit here for ten years or more before I find a use for them and immensely satisfying that moment is, too!

re-covering a chair seat

Changing the cover of a dining chair seat is a simple way of giving the whole room a new look, yet it requires only a small square of fabric. A set of chairs doesn't have to match – in fact, I prefer using three different fabrics on a set of six chairs. It helps if there is a linking theme or colour between the fabrics to bring them all together.

When you only need a small piece of fabric, it's possible to buy remnants of a roll at a very reasonable price. At a charity shop, you might find an old pair of floral curtains that are a little faded at the edges but with plenty of fabric in good condition. Small pieces of fabric can also be found on eBay – a fruitful hunting ground for adding to my personal store cupboard.

1 Using a tack lifter and a small hammer or a staple remover (depending on how the previous cover has been attached), take out the old tacks and then remove the old cover. Always aim the tack remover away from the body.

2 Using the old cover as a template, cut out a matching piece of fabric and place it over the seat pad, then turn the seat over so the underside is facing upwards.

3 Use a staple gun to attach the fabric to the centre of the longest side. Now, pulling the fabric tightly, staple it at the centre of the opposite side. Add a couple more staples at each side of these two attachment points before doing the same on the remaining sides of the seat pad, remembering to pull tightly as you go.

4 Finally, staple the remaining edges and corners in the same way. It may be necessary to snip the fabric at the corners in order for it to lie flat. For a neat finish, you can cover the underside of the pad by taking a piece of matching or plain fabric and cutting it out a couple of centimetres larger than the pad. Fold over the raw edges and staple it onto the base using the same method as before, pulling the fabric tight on each side as you go.

autumn recipes

The steady fall of the leaves, softening sun and shorter days call for warming bowls of soup, and while I haven't given up salads by any means, the ingredients have changed to include pulses and roasted vegetables. The season of comfort food has begun.

roasted butternut squash soup

One of the great things about autumn is the return of soup season. When the wind is gusting outside, the leaves are being blown from the trees and the skies have turned ominously grey, coming in to a warm bowl of soup and a hunk of bread is the most comforting thing. Butternut squash is the perfect vegetable for soup. By October the fruits have been picked and have spent time sitting on a table in the sunshine to harden their skins for storage in the larder, for months or until they have all been eaten, which doesn't usually take that long.

A variety of toppings can be added to the soup, from a spoonful of yoghurt (see page 188 for home-made) to grated cheese and a sprinkling of chopped parsley or coriander. A tablespoon of dukka is also a great addition, or even a little fried chorizo.

Serves 4

- 1 large or 2 small butternut squash, about 1.5kg (3lb 5oz) total weight
- 2 tablespoons olive oil
- 25g (1oz) butter
- 1 large onion, chopped
- 1 garlic clove, crushed
- 1 small green or red chilli (optional), finely chopped
- 1 litre (1¾ pints) vegetable stock
- 250ml (9fl oz) milk
- salt and pepper
- toppings of your choice (see recipe introduction), to serve

Preheat the oven to 220°C (425°F), Gas Mark 7. Line a roasting tray with nonstick baking paper.

Cut the squash in half lengthways and scoop out the seeds with a spoon, then chop into pieces roughly 4cm (1½ inches) in length. There is no need to peel them – the skin adds a lot of flavour. Place in a large bowl, add the olive oil, season well with salt and pepper and mix well. Spread out on the lined tray and roast for 30–40 minutes, or until the flesh is soft and the edges are beginning to caramelize.

While the squash is roasting, melt the butter in a large saucepan over a medium heat, add the onion and cook slowly for about 10–15 minutes, until soft. Add the garlic and chilli, if using, and cook for a further couple of minutes.

When the roasted squash is done, remove it from the oven and add to the saucepan with the stock and milk, then let it all simmer for 15 minutes. Remove from the heat and allow to cool, then transfer to a blender in batches to liquidize. It's important to liquidize the soup for long enough, perhaps longer than you think is necessary, to achieve a beautifully velvety finish. Sieving each batch as you decant it into a clean pan will also help it to become very smooth. Reheat gently and add seasoning to taste, then serve with your chosen topping.

spiced focaccia

We love this version of soft focaccia, adapted from a recipe of Sabrina Ghayour's. The spices give it a bit of oomph, and it is so simple to make. It goes well with a bowl of soup or dips and is also good with barbecued steak or chicken.

Serves 6–8

- 100g (3½oz) Greek-style yoghurt
- 250ml (9fl oz) hot water
- 550g (1lb 4oz) strong white bread flour
- 2 teaspoons fine sea salt
- 2 teaspoons caster sugar
- 7g (¼oz) sachet fast-action dried yeast
- 2 tablespoons cumin seeds
- 1 tablespoon ground coriander
- 1 tablespoon poppy seeds
- 1 teaspoon chilli flakes
- 2 tablespoons extra virgin olive oil

For the topping

- 150ml (5fl oz) extra virgin olive oil
- 1 tablespoon cumin seeds
- 1 teaspoon sumac
- a few thyme sprigs
- sea salt flakes

Mix the yoghurt with the hot water in a large mixing bowl to make a tepid liquid. Add all the other main ingredients and mix well until the mixture comes together into a rough ball of dough. If the mixture seems a little dry, add an extra tablespoon of hot water. Cover the bowl with clingfilm and leave to rest somewhere warm for 15 minutes.

Line a 25 x 35cm (10 x 14in) baking tray with nonstick baking paper. Transfer the dough to the lined tray and gently push the dough out from the centre to stretch it into the corners. Then make indents in the dough all over with your fingers. Cover with the clingfilm and leave to rise in a warm place for 1 hour.

Preheat the oven to 200°C (400°F), Gas Mark 6.

Remove the clingfilm and drizzle the extra virgin olive oil all over the dough, getting into all the indents and corners. Sprinkle liberally with sea salt flakes and the remaining topping ingredients and bake for 25–30 minutes until golden brown.

Remove from the oven, turn out of the tin and allow to cool on a wire rack for 10 minutes before eating.

a warm butternut squash and sweet potato salad

Just because we are now in the cosy season, it doesn't mean that I don't want to stop eating salads – they are an all-year-round staple of my kitchen. However, autumn and winter call for a little more warmth, so roasting the main ingredients provides that. For crunch and added fibre, I like to keep the kale raw.

Serves 4

- 1 butternut squash, about 600g (1lb 5oz) prepared weight
- 2 large sweet potatoes, about 400g (14oz) total weight, scrubbed
- 2 large red onions
- 2 tablespoons olive oil
- 1 tablespoon garlic granules
- 1 tablespoon za'atar
- 150g (5½oz) kale, such as cavolo nero
- 120g (4¼oz) couscous
- 1 teaspoon vegetable bouillon powder
- 150ml (5fl oz) just-boiled water
- 75g (2¾oz) feta cheese
- 75g (2¾oz) cashew nuts

For the dressing

- 200g (7oz) Greek-style yoghurt
- 1 garlic clove, peeled
- 1 lemon
- 1 tablespoon olive oil

Preheat the oven to 200°C (400°F), Gas mark 6. Line a large roasting tray with nonstick baking paper.

Slice the squash into rings, remove the seeds and chop into chunks roughly 3cm (1¼ inches) in size – there is no need to peel them. Chop the sweet potatoes into similar-sized pieces and place in a large mixing bowl with the squash. Peel and quarter the red onions, then cut each quarter in half and add to the bowl. Add the olive oil, garlic granules and za'atar and liberally season with salt and pepper, then mix until all the vegetable pieces are well coated.

Spread the vegetables out on the lined tray (keeping the mixing bowl, unwashed, for the couscous) and roast for about 45 minutes, or until the edges are starting to caramelize.

While the vegetables are roasting, wash the kale and remove the tough spines. It's best to do this by holding the stalk end firmly in one hand and pulling off the leaves with the other hand. You may need to start by ripping the first 1cm (½ inch) off the spine, then the leaf should come off cleanly. Roll up several leaves together into a cylinder and slice very thinly with a sharp knife.

Towards the end of the vegetable roasting time, add the couscous to the reserved mixing bowl so that it can absorb the residue of flavoured oil. Stir in the bouillon powder and just-boiled water, cover the bowl with a plate and leave the couscous to soak for 5–10 minutes.

Remove the roasted vegetables from the oven and allow to cool a little. Meanwhile, spread the cashew nuts out on a baking sheet and toast in the oven for 5 minutes.

To make the dressing, put the yoghurt into a small bowl, then grate in the garlic and the zest of the lemon. Squeeze in the juice of the lemon, add the olive oil and season with salt and pepper, then mix well.

Remove the cashew nuts from the oven. Fork through the couscous to loosen it, then stir a tablespoon of the dressing through it, add the kale and mix well. Place in a wide, shallow serving bowl, scatter the roasted vegetables on top and add the feta, crumbling it with your fingers. Roughly chop the cashew nuts, then sprinkle on top of the salad. Place in the centre of the table with the bowl of dressing for people to help themselves.

carrot cake

Perhaps the most comforting of cakes, this old favourite is perfect for autumn, and there are so many different recipes to choose from. Having had a child who didn't like nuts in anything, I left out the walnuts originally and it has stayed that way to this day, even though that particular child is now 30! I like to make this as one layer with the frosting on top, rather than with the frosting sandwiched between two layers, which can end up being too rich. Here is my version of the much-loved cake.

Serves 8

- 200g (7oz) light brown soft sugar
- 170ml (6fl oz) sunflower oil, plus extra for greasing
- 2 large eggs
- 200g (7oz) plain flour
- 1 teaspoon baking powder
- ½ teaspoon bicarbonate of soda
- ¼ teaspoon salt
- 1 teaspoon vanilla extract
- 1 teaspoon ground cinnamon, plus extra (optional) to decorate
- ½ teaspoon ground ginger
- 200g (7oz) carrot, grated

For the cream cheese frosting

- 30g (1oz) butter at room temperature
- 150g (5½oz) icing sugar
- 60g (2¼oz) cream cheese

Preheat the oven to 180°C (350°F), Gas Mark 4. Grease a 20cm (8in) round springform cake tin.

Place the first 3 ingredients in the bowl of a stand mixer and beat for about 1 minute until well mixed. Alternatively, use a large mixing bowl and electric hand mixer. Then measure the flour into a bowl and add all the other ingredients, except the carrot, giving it a quick stir. Add to the egg mixture and combine on a low speed. Finally, fold in the grated carrot with a spatula.

Scrape the cake batter into the prepared tin and bake for about 50 minutes, or until a sharp knife inserted into the cake comes out clean. Remove from the oven and allow to cool completely in the tin on a wire rack.

To make the frosting, beat the butter and icing sugar together in a stand mixer, or in a mixing bowl using an electric hand whisk, until well mixed. Then add the cream cheese and beat for 5 minutes. This may seem like a long time, but this is how you get a lovely light, fluffy texture.

When the cake is completely cool, remove carefully from the tin and spread the frosting on top, creating texture with the flat side of the knife so that it's not too uniform. Add a sprinkle of cinnamon to decorate, if desired, and serve.

winter

A new seasonal shift is taking place – the garden curls and shrinks into itself more with each successive frost, seedheads are left to overwinter for the birds to feed on, and the leaves have been raked into a heap to become valuable compost. Human life retreats inside the house, where a fire is lit at teatime every day. Winter has begun in earnest.

It may be the quietest season in the garden, but every day I put on my coat and hat to go outside. Sometimes I open the door and feel the sharp bite of the frosty air, and a brisk walk around the fields is all I can manage before my fingertips start to feel numb. I hurry back indoors for a warming cup of coffee and look out at the frosty brilliance from the comfort of a cosy armchair. These days are a chance to slow down, listen to my body and allow it to rest.

Now is the time to dream and make plans for the house and the garden, and for a few short weeks it is just that, a time for dreaming, not for doing. It's so important not to rush headlong into activity, especially at the beginning of a new year, but to give the mind and body time to recoup energy.

Right: This corner of the shed is a good spot to spend a happy afternoon. With the wood burner alight it soon warms up, and a blanket is nice for extra cosiness.

Reflecting quietly on what worked in the garden last year can inform and inspire me for the coming year's ventures as I sift through my thoughts and feelings in an unpressured way. Looking after myself like this allows me to prepare for action when it is needed.

Every day I will spend some time outside, breathing the fresh air deeply and turning my face towards the sun on the few days that it shines. Being out in nature is such a mood-lifter at a time of year that can be challenging, with its low light levels and dank, chilly days. I won't be gardening at this time but just quietly experiencing what is happening around me. Small changes are taking place even in midwinter, as in a slowly fattening bud, a catkin waving and the robin coming to see what I am doing in his garden. Getting outside is crucial to my enjoyment of these restorative days: to listen, look and ponder, and then to return to the warm seat by the fire.

January, the quietest month, is a time to reflect, take stock and make new plans. The new year brings the desire to clear away the clutter of Christmas and start with a clean slate and a clear house. Wrapping and packing away cherished ornaments, when done mindfully, can boost your mood, the feverish activities of pre-Christmas just a memory now. All of the natural decorations can be put on the compost, and the wreath rings and twine put away until they are needed. The house has been tidied, swept and dusted, and we are ready for the year to begin.

Left: Frost lies thick on the ground and it seems as if nothing could grow in the cold. But there is always something happening out of sight; soon snowdrops start peeking through and once again it is hellebore time.

structure in the winter garden

By the beginning of January the garden can feel stripped of colour and life. Texture is a vital part of creating interest in winter. There are the long grasses and seedheads from autumn, which can be ethereally beautiful when frosted. They also provide vital nourishment for our garden birds, and can be left for at least another month.

Topiary can be very useful for providing structure and interest in these months. The clipped shapes become focal points either in pots or in the ground. Topiary shapes are many and varied, the simplest being a ball at ground level. After that, you are limited only by your imagination. The great thing is that if you make a mistake, it grows back – as with an unfortunate haircut, you only have to wait a couple of months and all is well again.

Box is perhaps the most traditional plant suitable for topiary, although these days, with blight and box caterpillar moth, it feels brave to start creating something with it. Yew is another option, but that is strangely attractive to deer and so no good for us. I have used Portuguese laurel and privet to create umbrella-shaped topiary.

Beech provides an alternative colour, as it doesn't lose its browned leaves until the spring. It's important to clip at the correct time for each plant but this is generally between May and October. Never clip if there is a hint of frost in the forecast.

In the past I always used hand clippers to do my topiary, which was quite time-consuming, but then a few years ago my husband gave me rechargeable mini hedge clippers and they have changed everything. I positively skip out with my 'ladies' hedge clippers' (his description) and delight in the smooth finish they give, the result of which is especially pleasing on an icy winter's day as I gaze out to my topiary from the comfort of a cosy armchair.

Above: It helps to have repeated shapes in the winter garden for cohesion. Topiary works better if it is not in isolation.
Right: A variegated Portuguese laurel provides structure in winter and a shady place to sit on a summer's day.

what is growing now

When we do venture out into the garden, snowdrops are beginning to appear by the third week of January. One of the most recognizable plants and indeed most cherished, the snowdrop has so much charm and such fortitude to brave the icy weather. It is generous, too, multiplying yearly on its own. We can help it by dividing the plant at the end of the flowering season.

I like to plant up small terracotta pots of snowdrops to display in the house and on the table outside the kitchen window, where I can see them during the day. The shelves of the potting shed are adorned with small pots of treasures, quite happy to be planted out in the garden again once they have finished flowering. There are so many varieties of snowdrop – around 500 so far, a number that increases every year – and they inspire absolute dedication and even obsession in collectors. Known as galanthophiles, they compete to own rare varieties and will pay enormous amounts for a single bulb. I can't claim to have that sort of fervour but I do welcome with much joy their undeniable beauty in the winter garden.

Another winter gem is the hellebore, or Lenten rose, a plant that bridges two seasons and can flower for up to three months. Hellebores range in colour from snowy white through pale pinks to rich burgundies and on to virtually black. The leaves from the previous year need to be cut down so as not to obscure the new flowers. Cutting back hellebore leaves is one of the first jobs of the gardening year.

Left: Fair maids of February, also known as snowdrops, are a welcome sight when they start appearing in mid-winter.
Above: Snowdrops brighten up the potting shed windowsill. I will plant them out when they have finished flowering.

It can be achieved in small bursts to save your back and prevent fingers and toes getting too cold.

We might associate blossom with spring but there are a few small trees that flower much earlier than that and are well worth thinking about including in a garden. *Prunus subhirtella*, the winter-flowering cherry, is a real winter wonder with its delicate pink-tinged white flowers seemingly impervious to the weather. *Cornus mas* is another favourite of mine, with its shower of small yellow flowers – it greets me every time I step outside the front door and always makes me smile.

Winter is a quiet season in my vegetable patch, where there isn't a huge amount going on. Kale, the wonder plant, survives all weathers and doesn't mind being frozen solid. If I could only grow one vegetable, it would be kale, the saviour of many a meal. Parsnips also improve in flavour after a cold spell, even if digging them out of frozen ground can be challenging. I also grow salad in the greenhouse in the tomato beds, and this is enough to give us some fresh greens for our lunch every day.

Above: A small bowl of snowdrops can give so much joy. A pin frog in the bottom of the bowl holds them in place. **Opposite, clockwise from the top left:** The first hellebore to appear is always 'Naomi'; the delicate blossom of *Prunus subhirtella*, followed (below) by the glow of the *Cornus Mas*. The redoubtable kale, unaffected by a heavy coat of frost.

an outdoor table display of bulbs

A table full of pots of bulbs, visible from the kitchen window, is an attractive addition to the winter garden. It doesn't have to be large – a small round bistro table in a corner somewhere will do. It just has to be in a position where you can peer out at it and get solace from the knowledge that one day soon it will be abundant with blooms.

I like to use not only a variety of bulbs but also pots of different shapes and sizes, some of them terracotta and some metal. The smaller containers go at the front and the larger ones at the back, where I plant the taller bulbs. In the front are muscari and dwarf iris. Behind these are hyacinths and hellebores and then at the back are the narcissi. I might add a couple of evergreen ferns to provide texture and much-needed greenery, as well as a small pot of white saxifrage, which flowers even in the cold months. I like to keep the colour palette fairly simple and muted, but there are some fabulous richly coloured irises and hyacinths.

As for narcissi, my go-to varieties are 'Thalia', 'Erlicheer' and 'Bridal Crown'. Once you've planted them and topped the pots with grit to make them look neat, the waiting game begins, with emerging growth looked at daily and measured in millimetres. Still, it's an exciting moment when you spot the first tips poking through and you know that spring will soon return.

Left: A cat enjoys the sight and scent of the flower table outside the kitchen. Hyacinths are one of the delights of January, when there is so little else about. They are very adaptable and don't mind being split up and replanted.

A pot of three from a garden centre can be a very affordable way of bringing joy to the house and, to my mind, is vastly preferable to some tulips that have been raised in a hot house and flown thousands of miles to a supermarket.

bringing the outside in

While there isn't very much growth going on outside, I can bring the garden inside in the form of pots of bulbs. I enjoy searching for interesting containers for my indoor bulbs throughout the year, from vintage stores, flea markets or online auctions. Soup tureens are a great option for this, and because they are rarely used for their original purpose these days, they can be found fairly cheaply. Old ceramic jelly moulds are available for the same reason.

To protect furniture you do not want drainage holes in containers, unless you place them on a saucer – terracotta, also, being so porous, can mark furniture easily. It's important that the roots do not sit in water, so first place a handful of grit or gravel in the container. Follow that with some compost, and the bulbs can be placed on this. It is not necessary for them to be completely covered in compost, as they have enough food and energy in the bulb to see them through flowering. You can, however, cover the surface in moss (in my case, gathered from a low tiled roof in the garden), which looks nice and will prevent too much evaporation of moisture. I like to group several bowls together on a windowsill or a coffee table – they look elegant in threes. Water them sparingly, as they really won't need a lot to drink. Soon the room will be filled with the wonderful scent of hyacinth or narcissus, freshening the air and awaking the senses.

Planted in November, narcissus 'Paperwhites' are the first bulbs to light up the gloom of January for me. These are known as 'prepared bulbs', meaning they have had a period of cold storage so that when you bring them into the house they think it is spring and will flower within weeks. You can have them flowering for Christmas if you want, but I think there is already enough to dazzle at that time, and they come into their own in the spare, empty spaces created by the tidy-up after the festive season. After being planted

Right: White hyacinths in vintage French soup bowls. They sit on a tray placed on the sitting-room coffee table, where I like to have a rotation of potted bulbs in winter and a vase of fresh flowers in other seasons.

A TREE IN THE HOUSE · HICKSON
CREATE
Trees in Winter

CURATOR
HOME

TOPIARY
BEYOND THE MEADOWS
JASPER CONRAN COUNTRY

Flowers Every Day

THE SECRET GARDEN BY FRANCES HODGSON BURNETT ILLUSTRATED BY CHARLES ROBINSON
HEINEMANN
LOST CRAFTS
CASSELL
In Your Garden

in mid-December, by the beginning of January they are ready to glow, in the gloom of a month when joy can be in short supply. Place them on a windowsill in a passageway and you will catch their scent as you pass, being immediately transported to springtime.

You could also place a few small vases of paperwhites on a windowsill, with lit candles in-between. During these months, when there is so little in the garden to pick, using small bottles or miniature vases is a good way of creating an abundant effect. Bunching them together in a group or placing them in a row on a windowsill can be a charming way of displaying these tiny vessels, and more impactful than a single vase.

Paperwhites can get a bit leggy when grown inside so it's a good idea to support them with a few twigs, pushed into the pot when you first plant them. This provides a framework for them to grow through and will stop them flopping over the side of the pot.

Soon to follow after paperwhites are hyacinths. These bulbs are also treated so that they bloom early. After they have finished flowering they can be planted out in the garden, where they will continue to flower every year in the spring. I usually grow only white hyacinths, because winter has such a muted colour palette that I find white suits the outside world and feels more in tune with nature. I want to be soothed at this time of year, and while I always favour a restrained palette, it feels even more important now – a calm, contemplative time of year.

The final potted bulbs to flower are muscari (grape hyacinths) and then narcissi, by which time there is starting to be enough to pick in the garden for a spring vase and indoor bulb season is over for another year.

Left: Books and flowers – two things I often put together. Clockwise, from top left, are white muscari in the sitting room, hyacinths on the sideboard, the smallest vase of paperwhites in my bedroom, and a bowl of narcissi through the open kitchen window.

houseplants

When it's cold and grey outside, having houseplants can satisfy a yearning for greenery. They are such a good way of connecting us to nature and besides this they visually soften the edges of a room and help to make a home feel loved.

Houseplants are the easiest way to bring life to a room, and in winter they serve an important role for us, not only by providing greenery in the house but also by giving us something to care for and nurture. They are beneficial to our well-being at a time when it's natural for spirits to become a little low. Spending time in a room with houseplants can not only reduce stress and lower blood pressure but also improves air quality by removing toxins.

A favourite spot for houseplants in my case is the bathroom. They enjoy the extra humidity provided by the steam from a shower or bath, which produces the perfect conditions for them to thrive. Added to this they create an environment that encourages relaxation, for a much-needed moment of calm at the end of a busy day.

In my bathroom I have a row of houseplants on the mantlepiece, trailing varieties being particularly good as they have enough room to drape down very satisfactorily. Pothos and philodendron grow happily here and a Swiss cheese plant, plus a rubber fig, provide vertical interest. Ferns also enjoy the atmosphere in the bathroom; I have a hare's foot fern on my bath rack that grows so abundantly the soap and candle have to squeeze on at the end.

Another useful place for houseplants is a bookcase; the one shown to the left is next to a window that provides ample light even on the greyest winter day. Here I have the classic spider plant, a money plant and a round-leaved peperomia. Dotted among the books, the plants create a pleasing decorative look and bring this corner of my bedroom to life.

Above: In a light-filled corner of my bedroom, this bookcase is a great place for some houseplants. **Right:** The bathroom probably provides the best atmosphere of all for indoor plants. I place them on a mantlepiece.

Overleaf, left and right: I like to add pictures and photos to my shelves – mementoes from travels away and also ceramics. I have always collected jugs and often receive them as gifts, which I enjoy displaying as a reminder of that kindness.

BRITISH FERNS
FURNITURE

Ring of Bright Water
THE WRONG KIND OF SNOW
BROTHEL IN PIMLICO
ROY BROOKS
Howard Spring
ALL THE DAY LONG
GERALD DURRELL
I PLANTED TREES
ERNEST HEMINGWAY
FALLING ANIMALS
Garden Visitor's Handbook 2021
The Waters Under the Earth
JOHN MOORE
GAVIN MAXWELL The Rocks Remain
HEREFORDSHIRE
A SHORT WALK IN THE HINDU KUSH
Self-Sufficiency
UNDER-THE-HILL
JOHN FORSTER
THE TRIAL OF BEBE DONGE
Simenon
THE WHITE CLIFFS
Allan Jenkins PLOT 29
THE WOOD
JOHN LEWIS-STEMPEL
A NEW TREE BIOLOGY
THE WAY THROUGH THE WOODS
Nigel Slater
toast
SECRET WATER
ARTHUR RANSOME
GODS OF HOWL MOUNTAIN
TAYLOR BROWN
Yew & Non-Yew
JAMES BARTHOLOMEW
A LITTLE HISTORY OF POETRY
JOHN CAREY
Green and Pleasant Land
National Velvet
ENID BAGNOLD
Mary Oliver
UNDER THE TUMP
OLIVER BALCH
educated
TARA WESTOVER

the winter dining table

Every now and again it's fun to decorate the table for a special meal – maybe for family or friends, or just because a meal needs to be elevated. Perhaps a particularly difficult week has been survived or you just feel like celebrating being alive.

The winter dining table is all about creating a cosy, cocooning atmosphere. Rich, dark colours will help here, so a tablecloth in dark green or warm chocolate brown could be used, although I also like the texture of a wooden table, so it's by no means essential to cover this. Either several small candles or one large, cream church candle can look equally effective.

During these months evergreen foliage is among the rather slim pickings in the garden, but the muted colour palette suits the season, I think. The most abundant evergreen foliage in my garden is ivy, and the zingy lime-green clusters of flowers contrast well with the darker leaves. The trailing stems are winter stalwarts in arrangements, too. I add evergreen ferns to the ivy – making a simple display with a couple of shallow bowls and pin frogs doesn't take long.

For the thicker church candles I make mini wreath rings with bendy ivy stems, or I simply wind ivy round and through the group of candles, with its tendrils curling out from between them. Adding a string of battery-powered fairy lights will add to the soft glow and romantic atmosphere.

Left: I like to decorate the kitchen table, either when friends come round for a meal or just to celebrate everyday life. The leaves of ivy are so pretty. I gathered these, together with some of the plant's flowers, and a few pieces of evergreen fern; a table setting was then quick and easy to assemble. The buttery yellow candles were the finishing touch.
Above: A ring of entwined ivy at the base makes a simple yet effective decoration for a pillar candle.

building up a crockery collection

When we got married, we were given a collection of Portmeirion Botanic Garden china, which I loved at the time. Then at some point in the 1990s I decided that I wanted only white china – my Scandi phase, you could call it. I sold all the wedding china and started again. Then, about ten years ago, I made another seismic shift.

This time, I began a collection of handmade crockery, which gives me so much pleasure. Eating porridge out of a handmade bowl elevates a simple meal from fuel for consumption to a pleasurable event that starts your day the right way. Curling your hands around a handmade coffee cup is a sensual experience that acknowledges the work of both the coffee maker and the potter.

Of course, pieces made by hand are not in the same price range as something churned out in a factory, but you are paying for the love and care that has been poured into a piece. In any case, it's enjoyable to build up a collection slowly. A visit to a potter's studio or a shop selling handmade pieces is an experience to be relished. Ceramics are also often available for reasonable prices in online auctions, and even in charity shops.

Left: The glazed cupboard in the kitchen holds most of my collection. I'm particularly drawn to speckled stoneware.
Below: This unit, bought on eBay and stripped of its varnish, is a handy place to keep mugs for the many cups of tea I drink.

winter recipes

The crunch of frosted leaves underfoot, the low-lying sun and the bite of a chill wind mean we need food to warm us as well as nourish. Added to this, January will always be the month of marmalade-making, and then making a cake with that marmalade makes so much sense – a glow-up for the beautiful orange.

marmalade

One of my first tasks of the new year is making marmalade. I always use my mother's recipe for it because I enjoy continuing a tradition, and also it isn't as achingly sweet as bought jars. A strong zing of orange is the flavour of hope on dark winter days. As you make the marmalade, the scent that fills the kitchen is wonderful. I tend to cook it long and slow, rather than at a raging boil that steams up the windows and has the potential to catch on the bottom of the pan. Marmalade must be made from Seville oranges, which are much less sweet than eating varieties. They are available from early January, but the season is short, so don't leave it too late to search for them.

Makes about 3.5kg (7lb 11½oz) or 8 or 9 jars

- 1kg (2lb 4oz) Seville oranges
- 2 lemons
- 2kg (4lb 8oz) granulated sugar
- 2 litres (3½ pints) cold water

Cut each orange in half, removing any nub of stalk. With a small sharp knife, remove the pips to a side plate or small bowl and reserve. Cut each orange half into 4 and place in the bowl of a food processor. When you have about 4 oranges' worth, process in short bursts until you have chunks of orange in a size that you are happy with. You will probably need to do this in 3 batches. Do the same with the lemons.

Put all the chopped fruit into a preserving pan or your largest saucepan. Gather together all the reserved pips in a small square of muslin and tie up your little bundle with kitchen string, then place in the pan with the fruit. Pour in the cold water and leave to infuse overnight. Already your kitchen will begin to smell a little more exotic and springlike.

The following morning, place the pan over a medium heat and slowly bring to the boil, stirring occasionally. Let it simmer for about 20 minutes until the bits of peel are becoming soft.

While the fruit is simmering, put the sugar into a heatproof bowl and place somewhere warm, such as on the top of a radiator or in a very low oven – the warming oven of an Aga is perfect for this.

Once the peel is soft, carefully pour in the warmed sugar and stir until it has dissolved. Increase the temperature and bring to the boil. It may take 2–3 hours, depending on how fast the boil is, but when the temperature of the mixture reaches 104°C (219°F) on a food probe thermometer, it's ready to pot up.

About 30 minutes before your marmalade is due to be ready, preheat the oven to 120°C (250°F), Gas Mark ½. Wash 8 or 9 airtight jars, about 380ml (13fl oz) in capacity, and their lids thoroughly in hot, soapy water, rinse well in hot water and stand on a baking sheet, then heat in the oven for at least 10 minutes to sterilize.

Once the marmalade is ready, remove the jars from the oven and use a soup ladle and a jam (wide-mouthed) funnel to fill the sterilized jars with the hot marmalade. Carefully seal the jars with the lids, using a cloth to protect your hands from the heat, and leave to cool.

mood-boosting porridge

Getting up, peeking around the curtain and discovering it's still dark – January can seem a long month. Sometimes it can be hard to find the motivation to get the most out of the short, dark days. It helps to start the day with something warm, nourishing and sustaining for the whole morning, and porridge is the answer to that.

Porridge is winter fuel – it really is a hug in a bowl first thing in the morning. While it is cooking away slowly, I unload the dishwasher and put away dishes from the night before, the timing of which seems to coincide perfectly with cooking porridge – a very satisfying sort of multitasking.

Makes 18 portions

300g (10½oz) jumbo oats

100g (3½oz) barley flakes

100g (3½oz) rye flakes

100g (3½oz) sunflower seeds

100g (3½oz) pumpkin seeds

30g (1oz) milled linseed

30g (1oz) chia seeds

organic semi-skimmed milk or almond milk (optional), for cooking

To serve

yoghurt (see page 188 for home-made)

clear honey

Put all the ingredients into a large mixing bowl and stir to combine. Spoon the mixture into a 2 litre (3½ pint) preserving jar or other airtight container.

To make one portion of porridge, add a heaped 60ml (2¼fl oz) scoop or 4 rounded tablespoons of the mix and three 60ml (2¼fl oz) measures or 180ml (6¾fl oz) organic semi-skimmed milk to a small saucepan. You can use water, if you prefer, or a mix of water and milk, and almond milk works well too. Cook over a low heat for about 6 minutes, stirring every now and again. I like my porridge fairly sloppy, completely unlike the solid cake of the stuff I was given as a child, but if you prefer a slightly thicker porridge, then cook it for a little longer.

Served topped with a couple of spoonfuls of yoghurt and a teaspoon of (ideally local) honey for the perfect winter breakfast.

yoghurt

Dipping a spoon into a fresh jar of home-made yoghurt is a heady moment – the rich, creamy delight may mean that the shop-bought version never has quite the same appeal again. Having said that, it did take me quite a while to perfect the recipe, but there is so much advice online that, with a bit of delving, I soon found the solution.

The milk powder is a crucial part of the recipe, though the exact amount is a case of trial and error. If you can get unhomogenized milk, it makes even better yoghurt, but it's not widely available, and regular organic whole milk works just as well. I buy Greek yoghurt to use as a culture; this needs to be labelled 'authentic' and should be the full-fat version. It is possible to use a couple of scoops of the previous batch, but it does tend to go a bit wild, resulting in a slightly bitter finish that gets more pronounced the more you make.

Another tip: buying a digital thermometer with an alarm has been a game-changer for me, and has meant no more milk boiling over the edge of saucepans. I thoroughly recommend buying one if you are likely to leave the room at any point during the process!

Makes 1 litre (1¾ pints)

850ml (1 pint) organic whole milk

80g (3oz) skimmed milk powder

1 teaspoon clear honey

80g (3oz) full-fat Greek yoghurt

Pour the milk into a 1-litre (1¾ pint) measuring jug up to the 850ml (1½ pint) mark, add the milk powder and honey and mix together using a small metal whisk until everything is thoroughly combined. Pour into a saucepan and slowly heat until the liquid reaches 86°C (187°F).

Pour the hot milk into a bowl and leave to cool at room temperature until it reaches 42°C (108°F). Whisk in the Greek yoghurt until it is thoroughly mixed, then pour into a clean 1 litre (1¾ pint) preserving jar and seal with the lid. Wrap in a clean tea towel folded into thirds lengthways and place in a warm spot – the back of an Aga is perfect for this, but on top of a boiler or near the radiator would do, too. Leave for at least 8 hours and for up to 24, depending on how thick you like your yoghurt (the longer you leave it, the thicker it gets). Unwrap and place in the refrigerator to cool for a few hours before eating.

marmalade cake

After a couple of bracing hours in the winter garden, it's nice to come inside for a cup of tea and a slice of cake. I'm a big fan of the restorative qualities of four o'clock cake. Just at the time of day when energy might be flagging, sitting down quietly with a slice of something home-made gives me renewed energy for the rest of the day. A winter favourite is marmalade cake, and why not, when you've already got the key ingredient to hand, freshly made.

Serves 8

- 200g (7oz) unsalted butter at room temperature, plus extra for greasing
- 150g (5½oz) demerara sugar
- 3 eggs
- 1 teaspoon vanilla extract
- 200g (7oz) ground almonds
- 100g (3½oz) polenta
- 1 teaspoon baking powder
- grated zest and juice of 2 oranges, juice reserved for the syrup
- 4 tablespoons marmalade (see page 184 for home-made)

For the syrup

- 3 tablespoons marmalade (see page 184 for home-made)
- 75g (2¾oz) caster sugar
- reserved orange juice (see above)

Preheat the oven to 180°C (350°F), Gas Mark 4. Grease a 22cm (8½in) round springform cake tin and line the base with nonstick baking paper.

Beat the butter and demerara sugar together in a stand mixer, or with a wooden spoon in a large mixing bowl, until pale and fluffy. Add the eggs, one at a time, and the vanilla extract, and beat until fully incorporated.

In a small bowl, combine the ground almonds, polenta, baking powder and orange zest. Stir the mixture into the cake batter along with the marmalade.

Using a spatula, scrape the cake batter into the prepared tin and bake for 40–50 minutes, or until a sharp knife inserted into the cake comes out clean. Remove from the oven and allow to cool for a few minutes in the tin on a wire rack.

While the cake is cooking, heat the ingredients for the syrup in a small saucepan, stirring until the sugar has dissolved. Bring to the boil and then simmer gently for about 5 minutes. Allow to cool slightly.

Prick the top of the cake all over with a cocktail stick. Pour the syrup over and leave the cake in the tin until it is completely cool. This delicious cake is quite fragile and needs to be transferred to a serving plate with care.

the festive season

Creating a magical festive home using natural foliage, colours, textures and scents is a way of enjoying the season in an enriching and mindful way. Forging new traditions while embracing those that have meant something to us through the years will produce a Christmas home in which to cherish those we love, and will entice guests to enjoy the delights of the season.

For us, Christmas, a time rich in nostalgia, truly begins when my daughter appears on my doorstep for wreathmaking day. This is usually in the first week of December. Slowly I will decorate the house, adding a wreath, a small tree or just some fairy lights to a shelf until, bit by bit, the house starts to feel fully festive and celebrations can begin.

Some days are taken up with cooking in advance, in order to ease the pressure to produce meals over the holiday period. Other days will include meeting up with a friend for a bowl of soup, or even just a quick coffee. Nowadays I make a conscious effort to enjoy this time and not become overwhelmed by the pre-Christmas panic. By taking it one day at a time and not overloading myself with too many jobs, I am able to savour this run-up in a much more intentional way. After all, the to-do list always gets done in the end, and, by making time for quiet moments, just for myself, I have learned to relish what is a very joyous time of year.

Right: The colours of my Christmas. I like to use warm caramel tones as opposed to the traditional red, together with browns and greens, which are favourites of mine all year round and give a softer, calmer feel to the festive season.

TALES OF A WAYSIDE INN
WYE VALLEY
WILD ANIMALS
WILD FLOWERS
BIRDS
TREES
GEOLOGY

a foraged festive wreath

For an appropriately festive look, this wreath is made from foraged green foliage. You can use nothing more than foliage if you wish, as it will look stunning in itself. Or add pine cones, a ribbon or fairy lights. You could also incorporate bracken in the foliage, as its brown tones would look very effective, especially if pine cones have been used.

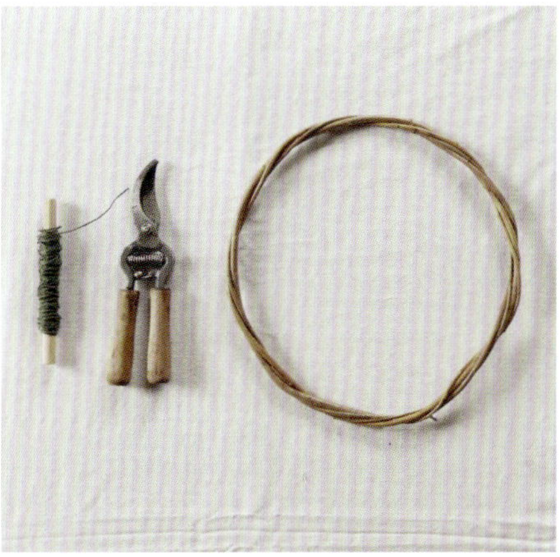

1 Use either a pre-made willow ring, as shown here, or make one yourself from vine prunings, which are easy to twist and wind round each other into a ring (see An autumn wreath, page 130). Collect your greenery. Here I've used fir, ivy, mistletoe, eucalyptus and holly with yellow berries.

2 Sort your greenery into mixed bunches of three or four stems. Each bunch should have sprigs of different lengths.

3 Attach the first bunch to the ring by winding florist's wire around the bunch a couple of times and then winding the wire tightly around the ring itself.

4 Working anticlockwise, place a second bunch next to the first bunch and wind it onto the ring, pulling the wire tightly to secure it.

5 Continue attaching the branches in the same way. The closer together the bunches are, the more fulsome the wreath, but a lighter, wispier look can also be effective.

6 Continue until the ring is completely covered. At the top, make a loop in the wire for hanging up the wreath. (You can add pine cones at this stage if you wish. Wind wire around the base of each cone, twist the wire and use it to attach the cone to the foliage.)

7 Finally, add a ribbon, either tied in a bow and wired in place, or simply looped around the wreath and left to hang, as here. You could also wind battery-powered fairy lights around the wreath for added sparkle.

decorating the house

I like to decorate using natural tones that are present in the garden at this time. The dark greens of evergreen foliage and the chestnut brown of wintering beech leaves mean that I lean towards terracotta and rust tones rather than the traditional red. Making your own traditions is part of the magic of Christmas, and a more natural look that connects the house with the garden seems to suit my style.

There is still room for sparkle, though, and lots of it. Although I love a completely unadorned small tree, I have selected spots in the house where the twinkle of fairy lights on a small Christmas tree can light up a dark corner and add a touch of romance. A small tree placed on a wide windowsill means that the tree can be seen from the outside, looking quite magical as darkness falls. I generally buy rooted trees, which can then be planted out in the garden or put into a large pot so that they can return inside the following year.

When using a more muted colour palette, texture is important. A bowl of pine cones gathered on walks throughout the year and placed on a coffee table can be very effective. Scent is also an evocative part of creating tradition – the nostalgic smell of a fir tree or a much-loved 'winter' scented candle can create an instantly familiar mood.

We usually put up our main tree midway through December. As with the rest of the house, I keep the colour palette muted, but this still includes much-loved decorations, some of which my children either made or gave me, while I collected others myself over the years. With Christmas jazz softly playing and a scented candle lit, decorating the tree becomes a joyful ritual, as we unpack old favourites from their tissue paper to hang carefully on the tree.

Keeping a connection with the garden outside can help to ground us and make the most of what can be a time taken up by consumerism. By stepping back from that and using nature to adorn the house and creating those decorations with our hands, we can create a calm and meaningful Christmas home in which to relish the joy of the season in a personal way.

Right: Nothing is more nostalgic than the sight of these light-filled houses twinkling through a window. **Left:** I like to have a small tree in the dining room; simply decorated, it adds a festive flavour to meals.

a festive mantlepiece

Decorating a mantlepiece for Christmas using material gathered form the garden or hedgerow can look very dramatic and impactful. The ingredients may be humble, yet the effect can be rather grand.

This is probably the final decorating task I will complete before Christmas, usually on the day before Christmas Eve. The heat from the fire below means that my display won't last that long. My container is an old metal baking tin, 46 cm (18 inches) long, which must have held the mother of all pies once upon a time, but is now perfect for this, very different job. I first fill it with scrunched-up chicken wire, held in place with narrow florist's tape.

Collected from the garden for this display were some stems from an evergreen pine, ivy tendrils and flowers, some eucalyptus and mistletoe. I also used brown bracken and some teasel seedheads, for contrast with the greenery.

After filling my container with water, assembly can begin.

Poking into the chicken wire stems of different lengths, I am aiming for abundance, with some pieces hanging down – ivy is useful for this – and some pieces sticking up. This is the time to be theatrical; I usually have to return outside for more foraging before I have enough. I carry on filling until the chicken wire, and most of the tin, is completely hidden. Remember to keep the container topped up with water. The whole arrangement can be misted with a spray bottle, too, if it needs it.

Walking into a room with decorated mantlepiece can summon the spirit of Christmas in even the most 'bah, humbug' of souls. It is one of the best ways of creating a dramatic festive display.

Left and above: Decorating the sitting-room mantlepiece, listening to Christmas music as I work, can be one of the most enjoyable festive moments for me, which when it is done signals the beginning of the holiday.

Overleaf: The wreath on the front door is fixed in place with velvet ribbon, which is looped over the top of the door and tied around a hook. The Christmas tree in the sitting-room, bought locally, is decorated in mid- December.

creating a festive globe

A dramatic way to introduce greenery is with a Christmas 'globe'. It does indeed look festive hanging in front of a window, so that it is visible from outside, or above the dining table. Winding in a string of battery-powered fairy lights creates a magical effect.

1 Using sturdy gloves, wrap chicken wire around itself, tucking in sharp ends, until you have a globe shape. Hang this temporarily with a piece of string either from the ceiling or in a doorway, so it is at a workable height.

2 Gather pieces of foliage. Here I have used trailing ivy and ivy flower stems, some yew, mistletoe and variegated euonymus. The pieces should be of varying lengths, unless you want a very neat final look. I prefer something a little less ordered.

3 Start poking in the stems, making sure they are secure in the chicken wire. This might take more pieces than you think as it's important not to be able to see any wire in the finished design, especially from the underneath, as that will be visible when it is hanging.

4 When you have enough foliage and are happy with the way it looks, thread in battery-operated fairy lights, hiding the battery pack in among the greenery. You could also add thin, tall candles, making sure the wicks are well above any foliage. Of course the lit candles cannot be left unattended, even for a second.

5 Swap the string for a piece of narrow ribbon and hang the festive cloud in the desired position. If it will be over the dining table, be sure to hang it high enough that it will not interrupt sight-lines for seated diners.

6 Occasionally misting with water using a spray bottle will help to keep everything fresh.

Right and above: My festive globe, equally at home in the potting shed and as a centrepiece to the festive table, where I have tied it to the base of the candle chandelier.

Overleaf, left: A star entwined with fairy lights and wound with ivy – hung on the wall, in a window or on top of the tree – is a beautiful way of creating something from foraged twigs. **Right:** Outside the shed on a snowy day.

the festive table

Sitting down to a meal with friends and family is a moment to relish during the holidays. Decorating the table adds to the sense of occasion, whether it is a sumptuous, theatrical display or a more minimal setting – both approaches can be effective.

A few cream-coloured church candles in terracotta pots filled with sand placed down the centre of the table can be a starting point. Surround these with a few pieces of greenery and you have a simple but effective festive table. For the day itself, or a larger gathering, you may want to create more of a display. Again, this can start with candles, but in this case more means more. I like to use a mix of different styles: a tea light in front of every place setting, as well as tall candles down the centre of the table. Something traditional, too – in my case, three wooden horses which were the centre of my parent's table and have now passed to me. Pine cones add a natural feel, but I sometimes also add baubles for a touch of glamour. The candelabra that hangs over the centre of the table receives the festive treatment, too: I wind ivy around it and add mistletoe to the frame the ivy has created, or, as shown here, hang a festive globe. Fairy lights are draped over the mantlepiece and candles glow on every surface.

Placing large candlesticks around the room creates a beautiful atmosphere, especially in the evening, when I won't use any electric light and the room is lit up with a cosy glow, creating a magical festive effect; this is much more conducive to conversation continuing late into the evening. After all the hard work, the season is there to be enjoyed. See page 211 for more inspiration.

Above: Each place is set simply, with a sprig of evergreen and either a fir cone or wooden snowflake decoration.
Right: The dining room is ready for its occupants.

festive season recipes

So much of cooking at Christmastime is based on traditions passed down through generations, and we find ourselves cooking the same meals every year. There is something comforting in knowing that we will be eating familiar meals loved and requested by the whole family. Towards the end of November, I get out my Christmas notebook, which details what I have cooked every year, what worked and what didn't, and I make tweaks, trying not to repeat my mistakes. Every few years I will discover and adapt a new recipe, and it will be proclaimed 'the best yet' and go into the book to be cooked like that for evermore!

mincemeat

Mincemeat is one of those things that are definitely worth making if you have the time. Commercial jars in which the overriding flavour is sugar are a pale imitation of what you can create at home. Full of fruity richness with a tang of ginger and spices, it will bring your mince pies alive and can be used in other recipes, too.

Over the years I have tried many different recipes for mincemeat in my search for the perfect mix – not too dry (or wet), not too sweet. A few years ago I discovered Gizzi Erskine's brilliant book *Gizzi's Season's Eatings* and I knew I'd found the perfect one. The following recipe, adapted from Barney Desmazery's blitz-and-mix mincemeat, has become a mid-November tradition. The mixture sits in its bowl in the kitchen for a day so that any passers-by can pause, have a stir and maybe make a quiet wish for the coming festivities.

Makes 2kg (4lb 8oz)

- 100g (3½oz) chopped candied peel
- 85g (3oz) stem ginger, plus 2 tablespoons syrup
- 50g (1¾oz) glacé cherries
- 100g (3½oz) fresh or tinned pineapple chunks
- 50g (1¾oz) blanched almonds
- 1 cooking apple, peeled and grated
- 225g (8oz) sultanas
- 225g (8oz) raisins
- 225g (8oz) currants
- 140g (5oz) shredded suet
- 225g (8oz) muscovado sugar
- 1 teaspoon ground ginger
- 1 teaspoon mixed spice
- ½ teaspoon freshly grated nutmeg
- finely grated zest and juice of 1 orange
- 150ml Cointreau or Grand Marnier

In a food processor, pulse the candied peel, stem ginger, cherries, pineapple and almonds until they are finely chopped, then tip into a large mixing bowl. Stir in the grated apple.

Add the dried fruit – the sultanas, raisin and currants – to the food processor and pulse in batches, then add this to the bowl.

Stir in the suet, sugar, spices, orange zest and juice and alcohol together with a couple of tablespoons of the stem ginger syrup. Mix well (a job the whole family can join in with, making a Christmas wish as they go!).

Spoon the mixture into sterilized jars (see page 185) and, ideally, leave in a cool, dark place for 3 weeks to mature before using, though I have happily used it after a couple of days.

mince pies

Of course, it wouldn't be Christmas without mince pies. In my house I always need to hide these when they are cooling – they never last long!

Makes 22

For the pastry

225g (8oz) plain flour

25g (1oz) icing sugar

150g (5½oz) unsalted butter, chopped into 2cm (¾in) pieces

1 egg

550g (1lb 4oz) mincemeat (see page 212 for home-made)

caster sugar, to decorate

In a food processor, put the flour, icing sugar and butter and process until the mixture resembles breadcrumbs. Add the egg and process again until the mixture forms a smooth, soft dough. Don't be tempted to add water, as this will make the pastry shrink during cooking. Wrap the ball of pastry in clingfilm and refrigerate for at least 30 minutes.

When you are ready to make your mince pies, allow the pastry to come to room temperature, and preheat the oven to 180°C (350°F), Gas Mark 4. On a floured surface, roll half of the pastry out and cut out rounds using a 7cm (2¾in) crinkle-edge cutter. Place the rounds in 2 non-stick bun tins.

Fill each pastry round with a heaped tablespoon of mincemeat – too much and it will bubble over and catch, but too little and they feel rather mean.

Collect up the scraps of pastry and put to one side. Roll out the other half of the pastry and cut out the tops, I like to use a star cutter but you can use any shape that will fit, or just a plain circle. Gather all the pastry scraps together and roll out again to make a few final pies.

Bake for about 25 minutes, checking after 15 minutes as you may need to turn the trays around to achieve an even bake. Once cooked, remove from the oven and sprinkle the tops with caster sugar before removing the pies from the tins as soon as they are cool enough to handle. Place them on a wire rack until they are cool; they can be stored in an airtight tin.

Christmas cupcakes

I've found that these days a whole Christmas cake is too big and too rich, and we are often still eating it by the middle of January. Of course, nothing is better than a hunk of fruitcake after a cold morning walk on frosty ground, but by January I find I'm hankering for fresher flavours. So now, instead of a whole cake at Christmas, I make mincemeat cupcakes, which provide just a mouthful of sweetness at the time of day when energy is perhaps flagging a little, before the evening games begin. You can scale the recipe up, or even down, depending on demand.

Makes 10

- 100g (3½oz) softened unsalted butter
- 50g (1¾oz) caster sugar
- 50g (1¾oz) dark muscovado sugar
- 2 eggs
- 125g (4½oz) self-raising flour
- 1 teaspoon mixed spice
- 175g (6oz) mincemeat (see page 212 for home-made)
- Sugar stars or cinnamon, to decorate

For the frosting

- 40g (1¼oz) softened unsalted butter
- 100g (3½oz) icing sugar, sieved
- 40g (1¼oz) full-fat cream cheese
- few drops of vanilla extract

Preheat the oven to 180°C (350°F), Gas Mark 4.

Cream the butter and sugars together in a large mixing bowl until pale and fluffy. Add the eggs and mix well, then sieve the flour directly into the bowl and stir. Finally, add the mincemeat and stir gently.

Spoon the mixture into cupcake cases to three-quarters fill them, then bake for 15 minutes, or until firm to touch. Remove from the oven and place the cakes on a wire rack to cool completely.

For the frosting, beat the butter with the icing sugar and cream cheese until light and fluffy, then add a drop of vanilla extract and mix thoroughly. Either pipe with a piping bag or just use a spatula to top the cakes with the frosting. Decorate with sugar stars or a dusting of cinnamon.

resources

STORES

Baileys Home Store
@baileyshome
Ross-on-Wye, Herefordshire
A really stunning store set in some renovated farm buildings, selling homewares and lighting. A visit here immediately fills all the senses, and is always inspiring.

Closet and Botts
@closetandbotts
Lewes, Sussex
A wide range of beautiful homewares, furniture and vintage finds, including an enticing clothing section.

The Country Crib
@thecountrycrib
Sherbourne, Dorset
Beautiful and useful things for the garden and home. A large range of flower frogs, plus gardening apparel made in their Dorset workshop.

Domestic Science
@domestic.science
Stores in Nailsworth, Tetbury and Stow-on-the-Wold, Gloucestershire
A beautifully created treasure trove of pieces for the home with a small vintage department in each shop.

ANTIQUE AND VINTAGE STORES

Lowlands
@lowlandsbristol
Colston Street, Bristol
A selection of mid-century furniture, old and new lighting, vintage wares and a fabulous ceramics section.

The Malthouse Collective
@themalthousecollective
Stroud, Gloucestershire
More than 80 dealers with a wide range of vintage and antique furniture including some mid-century modern items.

Station Mill Antiques
@stationmillantiques
Chipping Norton, Oxfordshire
Two floors with multiple sellers. Lots of old painted furniture, a great place for finding styling props for photography.

Wye Valley Vintage
@wyevalleyvintage
Pengethley, Herefordshire
Small but perfectly formed (see right), with carefully chosen vintage pieces, which are so cleverly styled they make it impossible to leave empty-handed.

ONLINE

Dante Ceramics
@danteceramics
Issy Taylor-Jones creates timeless functional stoneware, designed to elevate everyday rituals. I love her speckle glaze pieces.

Twinn Pottery
@twinnpottery
All pieces made by Faye Twinn who produces simple yet utterly beautiful homewares which will bring daily joy.

Goose Home and Garden
@goosehomeandgarden
A collection of vintage homewares and kitchenalia and a good garden section.

The Old Potato Store
@theoldpotatostore
Stylist Karen Barlow has unique pieces, all with a patina that shows a previous life and gives her ever-changing collection so much character.

Rowen and Wren
@rowenandwren
Homewares and furniture with craftmanship at the forefront, including terracotta pots and other garden accessories.

ANTIQUES FAIRS

Arthur Swallow Fairs
@asfairs
Antique, vintage and salvage fairs held in several locations throughout the year.

The Country Brocante
@thecountrybrocante
Decorative antiques fairs held in beautiful surrounds.

Malvern Flea & Collectors Fair
@b2bfairsltd
Three Counties Showground in Malvern, Worcestershire
These fairs are held ten times a year, usually on the first Sunday of the month.

FABRIC

Painswick Fabrics
@painswickfabrics
Painswick, Gloucestershire
An Aladdin's cave of discounted designer fabric, discontinued lines and end of rolls at half price or more. Many happy hours can be spent searching for the perfect piece.

Tinsmiths
@t1nsmiths
Ledbury, Herefordshire
Focusing on a large range of linens in muted colours; many are extra-wide. A beautiful homewares section, too.

GARDEN

Burford Garden Centre
@burfordgarden
Burford, Oxfordshire
Homewares, clothes, indoor and outdoor plants are all displayed in a beautiful way. With props such as vintage cars among the plants, a sense of theatre makes this a fabulous place to visit. There is also a food hall and restaurant.

The Nursery at Miserden
Miserden, Gloucestershire
@miserden
Part of the beautiful Miserden estate, which can be visited at the same time, with the added bonus of the Little Ginger Deli and Café for delicious cakes.

index

G

H

I

J

K

L

M

N

O

P

acknowledgements

Living in this lovely house feels such a privilege, but it wouldn't be possible without my wonderful husband, Thomas – my very own Caractacus Potts – able to fix all the many problems that come with an old house, whether it be the heating system or a hole in the roof. More than this, though, he manages to bring to life my crazy ideas, even better than I had imagined them. Need a bigger tomato greenhouse? He finds a 30-foot-long one on eBay, dismantles it, brings it home and rebuilds it, no problem. Want a shed with a veranda in the field? It's done! Thomas, I love and appreciate you more than I can say.

A huge thank you to my four children. To Ollie and Ed for their help with dismantling that greenhouse and for their tech support. Also my girls, without whose help this book would not exist at all. Cecily for endless technical help, and Daisy, who designed the beautiful endpapers based on a photograph of mine and who is always there in my hour of need. Thank you both also for fulfilling your modelling duties so willingly and with such good grace. For your fantastic support and encouragement right from the start of my Instagram journey to writing this book, I will always be so grateful to you both.

A big thank you to my friends, in particular Vanessa Simpson who gave me the confidence and encouragement to accept the challenge of writing a book in the first place. Also Leigh Chappell and Andy Heslop, two flowery friends, for their help and advice with arranging and growing flowers, respectively, and for coming to stay during a very hot summer week in order to chat all things book-related and to help me with the bouquet for a friend section. Thank you to Andrea Gilpin for being such a kind friend, too.

Finally, thank you to Alison Starling and everyone at Octopus books, including Juliette Norsworthy, for all your hard work in bringing this book to life. I really do appreciate the faith you had in me.

about the author

Harriet Thistlethwayte is a photographer and writer. She lives in Herefordshire, where she gardens and grows vegetables. A cook by profession, she is passionate about seasonality and using locally sourced ingredients. Her Victorian greenhouse has become a staple of her Instagram account, @yomargey, where she relates the trials and tribulations of rural living and her love for flowers and chippy old furniture. *A Country Style* is her first book.

For Thomas

First published in Great Britain in 2026
by Mitchell Beazley, an imprint of
Octopus Publishing Group Ltd
Carmelite House
50 Victoria Embankment
London EC4Y 0DZ
www.octopusbooks.co.uk

An Hachette UK Company
www.hachette.co.uk

The authorized representative in the EEA is Hachette Ireland, 8 Castlecourt Centre, Dublin 15, D15 XTP3, Ireland (email: info@hbgi.ie)

Copyright © Harriet Thistlethwayte 2026

Distributed in the US by Hachette Book Group
1290 Avenue of the Americas, 4th and 5th Floors
New York, NY 10104

Distributed in Canada by Canadian Manda Group
664 Annette St., Toronto, Ontario, Canada M6S 2C8

All rights reserved. No part of this work may be reproduced or utilized in any form or by any means, electronic or mechanical, including photocopying, recording or by any information storage and retrieval system, without the prior written permission of the publisher.

Harriet Thistlethwayte asserts the moral right to be identified as the author of this work.

ISBN: 9781840919707
ebook ISBN: 9781840919714

A CIP catalogue record for this book is available from the British Library.

Printed and bound in China.

10 9 8 7 6 5 4 3 2 1

MIX
Paper | Supporting responsible forestry
FSC® C008047

Publishing Director: Alison Starling
Senior Managing Editor: Sybella Stephens
Art Director: Juliette Norsworthy
Senior Production Manager: Katherine Hockley